Foreign Affairs
Europe's Furies

Foreign Affairs May 2017

Immigration, Terrorism, and Populist Nationalism

TABLE OF CONTENTS

TERRORISM

POPULIST NATIONALISM

Introduction

Gideon Rose

Only a decade ago, Europe was still heralded by supporters as a model for the world's future. It was like Walt Disney's original version of EPCOT writ large, the argument ran—an Experimental Prototype Continent of Tomorrow.

That was then. After a decade of economic crises and political turmoil, stalled halfway between national and regional sovereignty, Europe is no longer sailing proudly forward but drifting aimlessly close to dangerous shoals. The main risks to the continent now are political, with crucial elections approaching that will determine whether the EU continues or abandons its quest for ever-greater collaboration and openness.

To provide intellectual context in this time of choosing, we offer this collection devoted to three of the continent's crucial interlocking challenges—immigration, terrorism, and populist nationalism. Europe has absorbed large numbers of refugees from Syria and other countries in recent years, experienced repeated devastating terrorist attacks, and turned inward as a result. Foreign Affairs has been tracking each of these issues in real time, and we gather the best of our coverage here for handy reference.

In the end, Europe's center should hold. Austria, France, and the Netherlands have gone up to the brink only to pull back—even with a foreign thumb on the scales trying to engineer different outcomes. Other countries may do the same. But should current extremist contenders fall short, the problems that helped fuel their rise will remain. And how those challenges are handled will be the story of Europe's next chapter.

GIDEON ROSE is Editor of *Foreign Affairs*.

© Foreign Affairs

Destination: Europe

Managing the Migrant Crisis

Elizabeth Collett

Migrants look toward Macedonia through the Greek-Macedonian border fence, as a police helicopter flies by near the Greek village of Idomeni, March 2016.

The dramatic surge in the number of refugees and migrants that arrived in Europe over the course of 2015 should not have come as a surprise. For anyone paying attention to the civil war in Syria—as well as to the festering conflicts in Afghanistan, Iraq, Libya, and Yemen—it was clear that the crisis had been a long time coming. Yet the arrival of so many, and in so chaotic and desperate a manner, caught European policymakers off-guard. As more than one million people entered Europe, primarily by crossing the Mediterranean, the fabled solidarity underpinning the European project began to crumble. As some governments scrambled to construct makeshift reception centers in resorts and army barracks, others looked on with indifference, and still more did so with alarm. European politicians turned on one another, blaming those who had failed to manage their borders, those who had supposedly encouraged migrants with their hospitality, and those who had done nothing at all.

Last March, shortly after Croatia, Macedonia, and Slovenia closed their borders, shutting the so-called western Balkan refugee route, the EU struck a deal with Turkey. Ankara would take back migrants who had reached Greece and crack down on the migrant-smuggling industry that had taken root along the Aegean coast. In return, the EU would pay Turkey six billion euros to host the millions of refugees already displaced in the country and accelerate talks on visa-free travel for Turkish nationals to the EU and, in the longer term, on EU accession for Turkey. Numerous observers argued that the deal violated international law: Turkey, they said, was not yet a safe country for refugees, a claim strengthened by President Recep Tayyip Erdogan's crackdown on dissent and jailing of journalists and political opponents.

The only credible justification for the deal was that it was necessary to give the EU time to develop a sustainable internal response. Yet as the urgency of the crisis has ebbed, European officials have squandered the breathing room the deal gave them and reverted to the same policies they pursued before the crisis, including yet another attempt to reform the dysfunctional Dublin Regulation, which states that the EU country in which asylum seekers first arrive must weigh their claims and then either host or return them.

Despite all the frenzied activity by policymakers, thousands of migrants still try to cross the central Mediterranean each month, even during the winter; the EU is back where it was two years ago. Those displaced from the broken states of the Middle East and South Asia see few long-term alternatives but to attempt to reach Europe through whatever openings they can find in the continent's southeast. Meanwhile, the plight of migrants in Greece and Italy remains dire, with thousands crammed into overcrowded reception centers. If the deal with Turkey collapses, as many observers predict it will, Greece will be stretched beyond its still limited capacity to manage arrivals.

In some ways, it is not surprising that the EU's institutions have failed to rise to the challenge. On every issue, the union must reach consensus among more than two dozen states with divergent priorities and differing domestic political constraints. And EU politicians often seem more intent on settling scores between their respective countries than on crafting effective policy.

Will the EU remain committed to its founding liberal principles?

Meanwhile, policymakers can often forget the plight of the individual men, women, and children who have migrated. Two new books, both by journalists, attempt to redress this. The New Odyssey, by Patrick Kingsley, and Cast Away, by Charlotte McDonald-Gibson, chronicle the uncertainties and fears of the courageous, desperate, and sometimes foolhardy voyagers. They offer an important rejoinder to the idea, widespread across Europe, that such journeys are acts of pure opportunism. For many migrants, the decision to leave home, in the words of the Nigerian academic Aderanti Adepoju, exchanges "misery without hope for misery with hope."

In 2017, as crucial elections loom in the Netherlands, France, and Germany, the nature of the crisis will change. It will no longer be primarily a matter of numbers and state capacity. Instead, it will become a test of the European project's liberal values and of the EU's commitment to the international system for protecting refugees that many of its member states have championed for more than half a century. The EU will no longer be able to defer hard questions.

PEOPLE ON THE MOVE

To write The New Odyssey, Kingsley interviewed people in 17 countries, stringing together vivid snapshots of migrants, people smugglers, advocates, and, occasionally, policymakers. He returns throughout the book to the story of Hashem, a refugee who travels from Syria to Egypt, Italy, and, eventually, Sweden. As The Guardian's first "migration correspondent," Kingsley has witnessed hundreds of migrants' journeys over the past few years and has delved into the complex machinery of smuggling that facilitates them.

YANNIS BEHRAKIS / REUTERS

A stranded Iranian woman embraces her daughter as hundreds of migrants line up during food distribution at the Greek-Macedonian border, near the Greek village of Idomeni, November 2015.

The book brings home some of the mundanity of these lengthy voyages, but also the ingenuity of the travelers. In the western Balkans, Kingsley describes groups of young men sharing cigarettes and cracking jokes as they pick their way across the muddy terrain. Hashem, meanwhile, travels by train across northern Europe, hiding behind newspapers written in languages that he cannot read to escape the scrutiny of train guards.

Like Kingsley, McDonald-Gibson focuses on harrowing individual stories, but she does so in greater depth, following just five migrants on their journeys to Europe. One of them, Sina, is a pregnant Eritrean woman desperate to find a better future for her unborn child. A 24-year-old middle-class chemical engineer, she stands in sharp contrast to the media's caricatures of the migrants as impoverished and uneducated.

McDonald-Gibson's book thoroughly examines the forces that impel her characters to move and the personal conflicts they face as they make their decisions. An experienced foreign correspondent, McDonald-Gibson displays a strong grasp of regional geopolitics and the European policies and politics in which her protagonists are entangled. Her detailed narrative of the oppressive circumstances in Eritrea, for example, where the government forces people into indefinite military service, sheds light on a country that has become the single largest source of migrants from Africa but that Western media tend to overlook. Although the overall recognition rate of asylum claims from Eritrean nationals reaches around 90 percent in Europe, she notes that countries such as Denmark and the United Kingdom have started to dispute these asylum seekers' accounts of the conditions they face at home, and the United Kingdom now recognizes far fewer Eritreans as refugees. Meanwhile, in Italy, the conditions that greet asylum seekers are so poor that Eritreans try to avoid making their claims there. Governments have understood that generosity has a cost; indirect policies of deterrence are increasingly prevalent.

BALANCING ACT

In their attention to individual stories, these books indirectly illuminate why policymakers have struggled to resolve the crisis. To function effectively, immigration systems must create policies that are broadly applicable to all arrivals. But for the individual migrants themselves, with their widely varying experiences, blanket EU policies can seem arbitrary and authoritarian, especially when their fates often depend on the whims of particular officials. Balancing humanitarian responsibilities with the need to manage migration, while heeding the desires and fears of European publics, has become a defining challenge for the EU's liberal democracies.

A migrant after a rescue operation near the coast of Libya in the central Mediterranean Sea, February 2017.

Given these difficulties, people across the political spectrum have tended to oversimplify the apparent policy choices, boiling them down to an all-or-nothing decision: borders should be open or closed. At times, both authors, and particularly Kingsley, fall prey to this kind of thinking. In his policy prescriptions, for instance, Kingsley neglects to contend with some of the complex trade-offs that have made the crisis so difficult for officials to solve. He points out, correctly, that when countries close their borders, they often simply divert the flow of refugees rather than reduce the overall numbers—an example of the beggar-thy-neighbor policies that have defined much of the European reaction to the crisis over the past year. But like many who advocate a more welcoming approach, he also fails to engage deeply with some of the challenges posed by more porous borders.

Kingsley's primary policy prescription is that the EU can solve the crisis only by establishing legal means for would-be refugees and migrants to reach Europe, such as an organized system of mass resettlement. "Why make us do all this trip?" a Syrian refugee asks Kingsley near the border between Croatia and Slovenia. "Just organize it, give people visas so they can come on the plane. If you don't, people will keep coming."

EU politicians often seem more intent on settling scores between their respective countries than on crafting effective policy.

Kingsley is right that industrialized states should take in more people from countries overwhelmed by refugees, such as Kenya, Lebanon, and Turkey. But there's little evidence that such moves will deter irregular migration, especially in the short term. Kingsley ignores critical questions, such as how policymakers should choose whom to resettle, and he fails to grapple seriously with why Europe has not adopted such a policy already, preferring to blame Europe's inaction on the immorality of its leaders. And both Kingsley and McDonald-Gibson make only passing reference to security concerns and the awkward reality that terrorists have exploited unmanaged migration flows: two of the nine assailants involved in the Paris attacks in November 2015 probably arrived in Europe by boat. Such attacks do not justify governments' decisions to build walls or refuse asylum, but it is naive to not acknowledge the risks that come with allowing unidentified people to cross borders at will.

EUROPEAN DILEMMAS

The year ahead will be a difficult one for the EU. The deal with Turkey remains fragile, refugees and migrants remain in limbo on both sides of Europe's borders (recent estimates suggest there could be as many as 300,000 would-be migrants in Libya, for example), and voters are flocking to populist parties, driven in part by concerns over immigration. European policymakers will have to engage with some fundamental questions that they have so far avoided answering. Will the EU remain committed to its founding liberal principles? Can the EU preserve freedom of movement without reaching common ground on asylum policies? And what is the future of the global system of international protection for refugees, as some of the strongest champions of the current approach start looking seriously for alternatives?

Lifejackets in front of the European Commission headquarters during a protest by Amnesty International against the EU-Turkey migration deal, Brussels, Belgium, March 2016.

In 2017, the EU will have to decide whether, and how, it will continue to protect refugees. The question has become unavoidable for two reasons. First, several newer EU member states, notably the Visegrad Four—the Czech Republic, Hungary, Poland, and Slovakia—have effectively repudiated their commitment to the 1951 UN Refugee Convention. In a policy known as "effective solidarity," they have insisted that hosting refugees is for other countries and not for them—even though they accepted the responsibility to do so under the Common European Asylum System when they joined the union in 2004. McDonald-Gibson points out the irony of central and eastern Europeans vilifying asylum seekers even as their own countries' emigrant citizens are denigrated across western Europe, where millions of Czechs, Poles, Slovaks, and others have gone to work in the past decade.

But if EU countries fail to manage their asylum policies together, they will undermine the so-called Schengen system, which allows EU citizens to travel within the Schengen zone without passports. (Indeed, the relationship between asylum rules and the freedom of movement seemed so obvious to veteran EU officials that they thought it was unnecessary to formally clarify the link in the treaties that the Visegrad countries signed when they joined the union—an oversight they have come to regret.) If member states cannot trust one another to assume similar responsibilities with respect to border management, asylum, immigration, and security, they will be more likely to prioritize narrow national interests, as they did when they reinstated temporary border controls across the EU in 2015.

Second, those member states that ostensibly remain committed to protecting refugees, such as Austria, Germany, Italy, and even Malta, have begun to argue that the current system, in which asylum seekers must set foot in an EU country in order to claim protection, fuels the lucrative smuggling industry and discriminates against those who are too poor or weak to reach the continent. They have proposed "external processing": corralling people in neighboring countries and offering resettlement to those deemed worthy, thereby providing refugees with safer, legal routes to Europe. This approach has gained traction since the EU-Turkey deal, and policymakers are scanning North Africa for other partners with whom they can strike similar agreements, such as Egypt, Tunisia, and even Libya.

Although human rights groups have long advocated that the EU should expand legal pathways to Europe, they vehemently oppose external processing, arguing that to turn individuals away from Europe is both an abnegation of the right to claim asylum and a violation of human rights. In the model of external processing that European countries are currently discussing, non-EU partners would need to play a strong role in "pulling back" boats to their territory, hosting camps, and managing returns of migrants, a role that may prove beyond their existing capacity. Various governments, including Berlin and London, had made similar proposals over the past 15 years, but until now, such measures were always regarded as a step too far. Today, however, leaders believe that their political futures hinge on stemming migrant flows across the Mediterranean, no matter the diplomatic or financial cost.

Europe's leaders must not forget the principles of human rights that have underpinned their countries' asylum policies for decades.

If European countries turn to external processing, it may prove a watershed moment for the global refugee protection system. If Europe decides to focus on the resettlement of refugees as part of an external-processing model, rather than automatically assessing the claims of those who manage to cross its external borders, the system will risk becoming even more vulnerable to political pressure: a government could terminate a program at any moment. In the United States, for example, following the Paris attacks in November 2015, the governors of 31 states vowed to refuse any refugees, citing security concerns.

And external processing may not prove to be the panacea that Europe's leaders hope: the EU-Turkey deal—the template on which governments wish to base any future plans of this sort—suggests that the EU would struggle to manage such a system while maintaining the principles of international protection. It has little experience working on the frontlines of immigration and asylum policy and tends to view effective planning as a mere political afterthought. The experience of Greece, which has become something of a laboratory for external processing, has demonstrated that without the capacity or infrastructure necessary to manage thousands of people, the conditions can rapidly become inhumane. Even the Australian government, whose model several European governments have hailed, has yet to address the degrading conditions in its external-processing centers in Manus and Nauru, despite huge investments.

Any system for external processing would also depend on the willingness of EU member states to take in those refugees whom the union invited in to be resettled. The EU would need to find a way to compel European governments to maintain their commitments beyond a single political cycle; the reluctance of states such as Hungary to even contemplate hosting refugees suggests this would prove difficult.

But perhaps the biggest problem with external processing is that by striking expensive political deals with its neighbors, the EU would risk making itself beholden to states whose leaders may exploit their advantage. Erdogan's frequent threats to terminate the EU-Turkey deal, for example, have made European governments think twice before they criticize his increasing authoritarianism. European governments would need to announce clear redlines in advance regarding whom they will deal with, and on what basis, and preserve the ability to walk away.

External processing should not be condemned out of hand; the status quo—sea journeys that imperil thousands every day—is untenable, and the Common European Asylum System needs drastic reform. But the EU should not undertake the policy lightly: it must remember that any fundamental overhaul of asylum policy will require detailed planning, a long-term commitment to resettlement, and a recognition that such a policy will yield broader geopolitical consequences. And Europe's leaders must not forget the principles of human rights that have underpinned their countries' asylum policies for decades—and that lie at the core of the European project itself.

ELIZABETH COLLETT is Founding Director of the Migration Policy Institute Europe and a Senior Adviser to MPI's Transatlantic Council on Migration. Follow her on Twitter @migrationliz.

Directive 51

How Europe Pushes Migrants Onto Boats

Dimi Reider

A migrant is rescued by an Italian Navy helicopter in the area where his boat sank in the Mediterranean Sea, August 11, 2015.

In all likelihood, the past month will be remembered as a turning point in the European migration drama. Germany has effectively suspended Dublin II, the EU treaty that compels asylum seekers to register in the first European country in which they arrive, for Syrian refugees. Meanwhile, it has pledged not to cap the number of refugees it accepts, daring other European countries to step up.

Across Europe, Germany's sudden openhandedness is outmatched only by that of the wider public, from football clubs to private citizens, who have given millions of euros' worth of food, clothing, and shelter. For these people, one image has come to symbolize the crisis: the photograph of a three-year-old boy, Aylan Kurdi, slumped lifeless in the Turkish surf. It was both shocking and familiar. For years, the public has absorbed reports of refugees dying in overcrowded, barely seaworthy boats launched across the Mediterranean Sea.

And such images—regardless of civilian solidarity, renegotiation of quotas, or even a comprehensive suspension of Dublin II—will continue to pour in. People-smugglers will still charge thousands of dollars to pack desperate migrants on rickety boats. This is because the main reason that migrants choose boats, EU Directive 51/2001/EC, is not up for amendment or, at this point, even for debate.

ALKIS KONSTANTINIDIS / REUTERS

A refugee raises a child into the air as Syrian and Afghan refugees are seen on and around a dinghy that deflated before reaching the Greek island of Lesbos, September 13, 2015.

The EU directive was passed in 2001. Put simply, it states that carrier companies—whether airlines or ship lines—are responsible for ensuring that foreign nationals wishing to travel to the European Union have valid travel documents for their destination. If such travelers arrive in the EU and are turned away, the airlines are obligated to foot the bill for flying them home. The airlines can also be penalized between 3,000 and 5,000 euros per infraction. To avoid the fines, airlines have become diligent about preventing anyone without the proper passports or visas from getting on their planes.

Aimed at combatting illegal immigration, the directive does seem to make an exception for asylum seekers: "the application of this Directive," runs Clause 3, "is without prejudice to the obligations resulting from the Geneva Convention relating to the Status of Refugees." But airline staff is not qualified to examine the claims refugees, and the companies prefer to err on the side of caution. In practice, the caveat amounts to little more than lip service.

The EU and its member states need to take responsibility for examining refugee claims, instead of leaving it to airlines.

Indeed, thanks to the directive, the European Union has been able to relieve itself of the responsibility of examining the claims of most asylum seekers, shifting the burden onto private companies. The net effect is that the first filtering of refugees, instead of being handled by trained case officers, is generally left to check-in clerks, who are instructed by their companies to refuse travel to anyone not reasonably certain to be allowed to enter the European country of their destination. This acts as an automatic deterrent—and it drives people onto the smuggler boats. There is no other reason for families to pay thousands of euros for room on a floating death trap rather than a few hundred euros for seats on a short and convenient flight.

If Europe is serious about preventing more deaths in the Mediterranean, it needs to scrap the directive, or at least replace it with a more humane and equitable arrangement. For one, the EU and its member states need to take responsibility for examining refugee claims, instead of leaving it to airlines. The EU also needs to lift the penalties on airlines that bring refugees into Europe. Finally, the costs of deportations—when necessary—should be picked up, or at least shared, by the member states and the EU.

The removal of the restrictions on air travel would, potentially, increase the number of people lining up to claim asylum. Larger questions of the right to asylum and free movement aside, Europe should be able to cope with such an increase. Germany is already removing caps on the number of refugees it is willing to accept and promising to massively decrease the processing time for asylum requests. Other member states can follow suit, setting up speedier procedures for the examination of asylum requests and, if necessary, deportation.

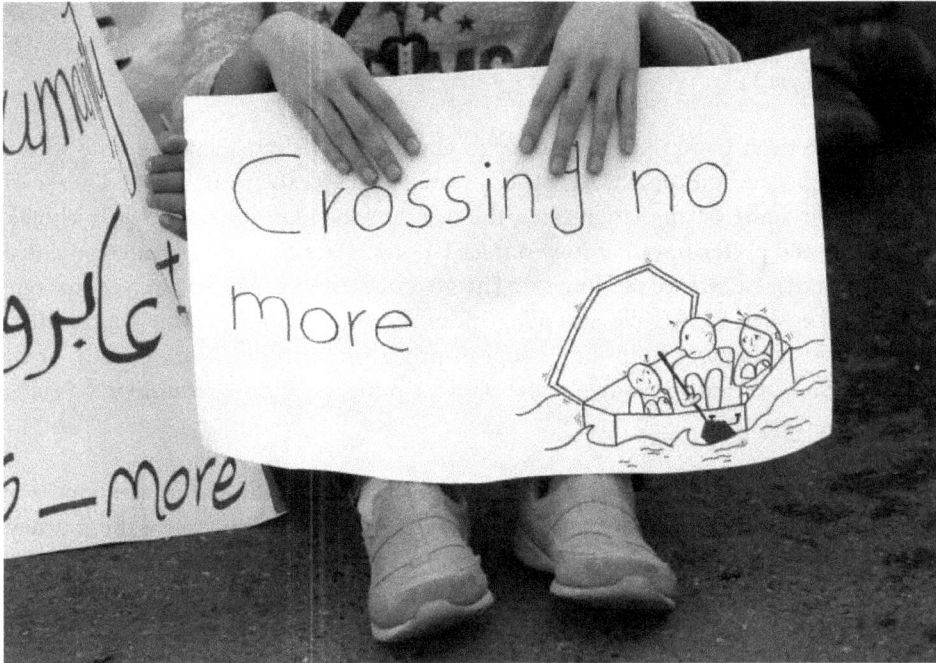

A Syrian migrant holds a banner reading "Crossing no more" as other migrants wait for buses at the main bus station in Istanbul, Turkey September 16, 2015.

The EU can back up member countries by setting up a Europe-wide infrastructure for initial filtering of claims on arrival—filtering done by trained and publicly accountable case officers, not by airline check-in clerks—and a shared European fund to cover deportation costs. Such a system would also significantly increase documentation, control, and follow-up of cases: it is easier to register and keep track of individuals arriving in an airport than of people landing on empty beaches and trying their best to stay under the radar until they reach a preferred destination of asylum. As an alternative, the EU could set up primary processing facilities in a safe country outside the EU, and the guarantee of hazard-free passage there for claimants—although it is difficult to see which country would shoulder the burden of becoming the union's bottleneck.

To be sure, these options would require generous funding; but then again, they would render proposed military campaigns against smuggler strongholds unnecessary. European officials have been circumspect about the projected costs of such a campaign, but the sheer scale of it and the involvement of navies and air forces suggest that it would be a costly one. With the rug pulled out from under the smuggling trade, conversely, funds could be channeled from war chests toward a more responsible and sustainable solution. This would also incur a much smaller cost in human lives than a military campaign. (Indeed, for now, the idea of destroying smuggler fleets before migrants board the boats and going after the more notorious smuggling gangs is moot anyway, after this spring's drowning of hundreds of refugees in a single incident off the Italian coast.)

The European Union has the power to eliminate the smuggling economy with a stroke of a pen. Abolishing 51/2001/EC would also pull the teeth out of Dublin II and even lift some of the strain from the negotiations over quotas: given a choice, refugees would prefer traveling to wealthier EU countries that offer greater potential for a new start, not Greece or Hungary. The governments adamantly opposed, for one reason or another, to actually accepting more refugees can make their contribution to the effort by helping fund the European processing and deportation fund, or by putting money toward providing a new start for refugees settling in more welcoming parts of Europe.

The changes happening inside Europe are crucial, and will go a tremendous way toward securing and improving the lives of those refugees who survive the journey. The deeper challenges of bringing freedom of movement and civil rights up to speed with a globalized, interconnected world will still be there, and will probably occupy us all for a generation to come. But if Europe wants to stop people dying by the thousands in the Mediterranean, it's not enough to be waiting ashore with blankets, or even to send rescue ships. If Europe wants people to stop drowning, it needs to let them fly.

DIMI REIDER is an Israeli journalist and blogger. He is an Associate Policy Fellow at the European Council on Foreign Relations and a co-founder of +972 Magazine.

© Foreign Affairs

The Return of No-Man's Land

Europe's Asylum Crisis and Historical Memory

Tara Zahra

A seucrity fence topped with razor wire is seen near the makeshift camp called "The New Jungle" in Calais, France, September 20, 2015.

In mid September, around 1,000 refugees were reportedly stranded on the border between Hungary and Serbia, with neither state willing to grant them asylum. The return of a "No-Man's Land" on Eastern European soil is yet another disturbing reminder of how history can repeat itself. No-Man's Land was last seen in Eastern Europe in 1938, when governments played a sick game of ping-pong with unwanted Jewish refugees, shunting them back and forth across state borders.

In one infamous incident in 1938, the Polish government passed legislation that stripped most Polish Jews living outside Poland of their Polish citizenship. Three days before the measure took effect, on October 28, 1938, Nazis rounded up 17,000 Polish Jews living in Nazi Germany and attempted to deport them to Poland. Poland promptly closed its borders. Throughout November, thousands of people were thus caught in limbo between the Polish and German border near Zbąszyń. They were housed in miserable tents, barracks, and condemned military stables—or else were left to freeze outdoors, exposed to the elements.

Hannah Arendt, the century's most famous theorist of refugeedom (and a refugee herself), explained such scenes as a symptom of the interwar obsession with national sovereignty. The state, "insisting on its sovereign right of expulsion... smuggled its expelled stateless into the neighboring countries, with the result that the latter retaliated in kind." The consequences, she wrote in her book The Origins of Totalitarianism, "were petty wars between the police at the frontiers, which did not exactly contribute to good international relations, and an accumulation of jail sentences for the stateless, who, with the help of the police of one country, had passed 'illegally' into the territory of another."

A Jewish family prior to being deported from Slovakia, 1942.

Such "petty wars" broke out along frontiers across Eastern Europe in 1938. On April 16, for example, Jewish residents of the Burgenland in Austria, on the border with Hungary (the very border to which the Austrian government is currently deploying 2,200 troops) were driven from their apartments, robbed of their possessions and identity papers, and dumped on a Danube island that belonged to Czechoslovakia. The Czechoslovak government deported them on the same day, to the purgatory between the borders of Austria, Czechoslovakia, and Hungary. The refugees spent three days trapped in a triangle of bayonets from three states. Finally the Jewish community of Bratislava, Slovakia devised an impromptu solution. They rented a tugboat that was stationed on the Hungarian coast of the Danube, and took aboard 68 refugees with a plan to travel down the river until they found somewhere to dock. No country would allow the tugboat to land, however. The refugees remained on the boat for three months while Jewish organizations attempted to find a sanctuary.

LOW MOBILITY

Today, No-Man's Lands, border checks, and internment camps are reappearing, and many of those countries that produced a lion's share of Europe's refugees in the twentieth century seem unable to avoid repeating their mistakes. The jubilant celebrations of a borderless Europe that accompanied the dismantling of the Iron Curtain and the expansion of the European Union have reverted to old demands for barbed wire fences.

ANTONIO BRONIC / REUTERS

Migrants walk towards the Hungarian border after arriving at the train station in Botovo, Croatia, September 23, 2015.

Today's scenes of desperate refugees (and human indifference) in Eastern Europe certainly seem eerily familiar to anyone with a superficial knowledge of Europe's twentieth century history. In 1937, the stateless (previously Austrian) Jewish writer Joseph Roth aptly described what he called the "metaphysical affliction" of refugeedom. "You're a transient and you're stuck, a refugee and a detainee; condemnded to rootlessness and unable to budge." Or, in the words of one refugee stranded in Hungary today, "Why is Hungary doing this anyway? We don't want to stay there. I want to go to the Netherlands, maybe Germany. Now I'm stuck here."

Perhaps less familiar is the long and deep history of Eastern European ambivalence toward refugees and toward mobility in general. This hostility has often been linked to an Eastern European preference for national homogeneity and national self-determination, and to Eastern Europe's own perceived status on the margins of Europe.

Since the end of the Cold War, Western Europeans and have assumed an inherent link between mobility and freedom. In 1989, nothing symbolized the failed promise of socialism so profoundly as the barbed wire and watchtowers that imprisoned citizens in their own states. When the Berlin Wall came tumbling down on November 9, 1989, commentators insisted that East Berliners were not simply crossing from East to West, they were also moving from captivity to freedom. As crowds of dazed East Germans wandered the streets of West Berlin for the first time in 28 years, Tom Brokaw declared, "Tonight in Berlin, it is 'Freedom night'…Thousands of East Berliners have been crossing into freedom all day long."

The unification of Germany and the expansion of the European Union to include former Eastern bloc countries in 2004 and 2007 were supposed to represent the realization of the basic principle of mobility as freedom, and that upheld freedom of movement as a "human right."

In reality, however, the past 25 years have been exceptional in European history. The much-vaunted freedom of mobility within Europe's Schengen Zone has always been dependent on the defensive barriers circling Europe's edges. Even during the Cold War, Western countries (including the United States) were typically only happy to uphold a right to asylum as long as only a few people could actually apply for it. As soon as refugees actually began to arrive, Western governments and popular opinion often turned against newcomers, questioning whether they were "bona fide" refugees or merely opportunistic "economic migrants."

Eastern Europe's history of ambivalence toward refugees was born at the very moment the region first began to produce refugees in massive numbers. The first major refugee crisis in Eastern Europe began with the Balkan wars of 1912–13, but reached astronomic proportions with the collapse of the Austrian, Russian, and Ottoman Empires in 1917–18, which together produced upward of three million refugees. The dissolution of Europe's great land empires set the stage for the subsequent refugee crises of the twentieth century, since Eastern Europe's new nation-states were founded on the fiction that national homogeneity was the essential precondition for a modern, democratic state. New restrictions on mobility in Western Europe (with the exception of France) and North America after World War I exacerbated the situation. The United States, which had absorbed several million migrants from Eastern and Southern Europe in the decades before the First World War, effectively shut its gates to immigration from those areas after World War I. In Arendt's words, what was "unprecedented" for refugees after 1918 was "not the loss of a home but the inability to find a new one."

Although the Austrian government did not actively deport Hungarians, Austrian diplomats and government officials made it clear from the outset that their hospitality had an expiration date

---

Such difficulties persisted in the coming decades. In 1956, for example, 180,000 Hungarian refugees descended on Austria in the aftermath of the failed Hungarian uprising against the Soviet Hungarian People's Republic. At first, Austrians tended to welcome the refugees with open arms. As time wore on, however, and greater numbers remained in camps and settled into life in Austrian towns and cities, Hungarian refugees from Communism were saddled with negative stereotypes. They were specifically accused of being work-shy freeloaders and economic opportunists, who had overstayed their welcome and abused the generosity of their hosts. Although the Austrian government did not actively deport Hungarians, Austrian diplomats and government officials made it clear from the outset that their hospitality had an expiration date. Hungarian exiles were strongly encouraged to move on to other countries for permanent resettlement. In a 1957 speech, Interior Minister Oskar Helmer proclaimed, "It is no longer acceptable that by virtue of its geographic position, Austria is condemned to bear the major burden of the refugee problem."

In the aftermath of the Hungarian crisis, the number of individuals who fled across the border from Yugoslavia into Austria also multiplied, as did the number of refugees whose asylum claims were rejected. In 1957, around one-fourth of Yugoslav applicants for asylum were issued deportation orders. The reasons for rejection were often arbitrary and inconsistent. One Yugoslav refugee was turned back on the grounds that "if all of the anti-Communists flee, who will remain behind in the country to fight the Communists?"

A migrant family waits to board buses on a field near the village of Babska, Croatia, September 23, 2015.

Most asylum-seekers were simply turned away because Austrian authorities insisted that they were "economic" and not "political" migrants. The criteria for distinguishing between the two remained unclear, however. A refugee who "made a good impression and has worked hard," and another who had "worker's hands" were granted asylum. A less fortunate candidate was rejected on the grounds that he was a "heavy smoker who has not worked much." In reality, since the very moment that the "refugee" was defined in international law, the distinction between "refugees" and "economic migrants" has been malleable in practice, and often used to willfully exclude individuals considered "undesirable" from a political, cultural, or economic perspective.

Contrary to popular belief, it was not only Western restrictions on immigration that ended mobility from and within Eastern Europe; it was also the efforts of East European governments themselves to immobilize their own populations. In particular, the more Eastern Europe's governments sought to keep out or to deport national, religious, or linguistic minorities (culminating in the expulsion of millions of German-speakers after World War II), the more they restricted the movement of their "own" citizens, who were needed to replace the labor of expelled or murdered minorities. Ethnic cleansing and border control were flip sides of the same coin. The more homogenous Eastern Europe's populations became, the more the movement of "valuable" national citizens was restricted. Czechoslovakia, for example, actually banned all foreign travel, including trips to visit friends and family in 1947—before the

Communists seized power. Communists merely radicalized restrictions on mobility that were often first introduced by democratic governments.

Having won freedom of movement, Eastern Europeans today appear to be most invested in erecting and maintaining an Iron Curtain around the continent's edges.

In yet another parallel to today's refugee crisis, Eastern European governments also justified restrictions on mobility in the name of "protecting" their citizens from exploitation abroad, fearing that East Europeans might become the "slaves" or "coolies" of the twentieth century. They often blamed mass migration itself on emigration agents—denounced as "traffickers" and "smugglers"—who supposedly fooled naïve migrants into leaving home and robbed and cheated them en route. There was little acknowledgement of the fact that escalating border controls and policing only increased the demand for the services of smugglers and agents.

IRON CURTAIN

Today, Eastern Europeans enjoy unprecedented freedom to move within Europe's borders, at the expense of those outside them. They have finally achieved a longstanding (but precarious) dream: that of being, more or less, accepted as "white" Europeans, officially guaranteed the same rights and privileges as Western European migrants. In contemporary debates, East Europeans are often praised as the "good" immigrants, in rhetorical opposition to those from outside Europe (especially non-white or non-Christian migrants), whose capacity to assimilate is continuously questioned. Former British Conservative Party Chairman and Member of Parliament Norman Tebbit declared in September 2013 that British citizens should not fear migrants from Eastern Europe. "We don't have much of a problem with people like the Poles, the Czechs, the Slovaks…they're not the problem," he insisted. "The bigger problem that is caused in our cities is caused by immigrants from the Third World who have got no intention of integrating here…They are people who left their country, came here and are trying to recreate their country in our country."

Having won freedom of movement, Eastern Europeans today appear to be most invested in erecting and maintaining an Iron Curtain around the continent's edges. Freedom of mobility, in the view of anti-refugee activists, should remain the exclusive privilege of Christian "Europeans." This may seem like a great historical irony, but it is consistent with a long history of linking popular sovereignty to national homogeneity; ambivalence toward migration itself; and Eastern Europeans' own precarious position within the European community. The fundamental tensions between a proclaimed "human right" to exit and the principle of national sovereignty may never be resolved, since states will continue to insist on the right to control their borders. And yet Europeans should be mindful of a past that has demonstrated that walls only create an illusion of security. Decades of experience show that the creation of a No-Man's Land erodes the freedoms of those on all sides of the fences that surround it.

TARA ZAHRA is Professor of East European History at the University of Chicago.

© Foreign Affairs

A Self-Interested Approach to Migration Crises

Push Factors, Pull Factors, and Investing In Refugees

Michael A. Clemens and Justin Sandefur

Afghan refugees seek shelter at a metro station during a rain storm in Victoria Square in central Athens, September 26, 2015.

Nations frequently help migrants fleeing crisis. They help out of generosity—generosity that quickly wears thin. What would they do if they acted instead from stark self-interest? Consider András Gróf, a refugee who arrived illegally in Austria after crossing the Hungarian border with a smuggler and then running through a swampy field under cover of darkness. He came without his family, without a college degree, without assets beyond 20 dollars. Back home, he had watched soldiers arrive, first to rape his mother, later to conscript young men like him. So András fled for the same reason that so many others leave the Middle East and Africa; whether or not there was an imminent threat to his life, the future in his country looked hellish.

András didn't arrive in Austria in 2015. He fled Hungary with 200,000 other refugees in 1956. But the global response to that earlier wave of (many non-Christian, mostly unskilled) refugees pouring into Western Europe shows a way forward for the international community today.

In an act of apparent generosity, 37 countries—from Venezuela to New Zealand—came together to resettle almost all of the refugees that resulted from the Hungarian Revolution of 1956. András went to the United States. Ten years later, under the new name of Andy Grove, he became a co-creator of Intel Corporation. Later Time magazine's Person of the Year as Intel's path-breaking CEO, he helped create an American industry of immeasurable economic and strategic importance. Other Hungarians in the same wave, who likewise arrived as unaccomplished young men, became artists (the great cinematographer László Kóvacs) and captains of industry (Steve Házy). More than 40,000 others became less-visible colleagues, neighbors, and spouses of Americans, strengthening and enriching the country vastly more than the assistance they got.

Grove's story reveals some larger truths. Recent research overturns the standard narrative: that addressing migration crises mainly means curtailing the conflict and poverty that "push" migrants away from home, and slashing the excessive generosity that "pull" them into other countries. Instead, pragmatic and self-interested policymakers should consider that they often waste resources when trying to reduce push factors, and they can spark an inhumane and inefficient race to the bottom by acting individually to reduce pull factors. Through broad international cooperation to get people out of camps and into the labor force, though, they can transform refugees from a burden into an investment.

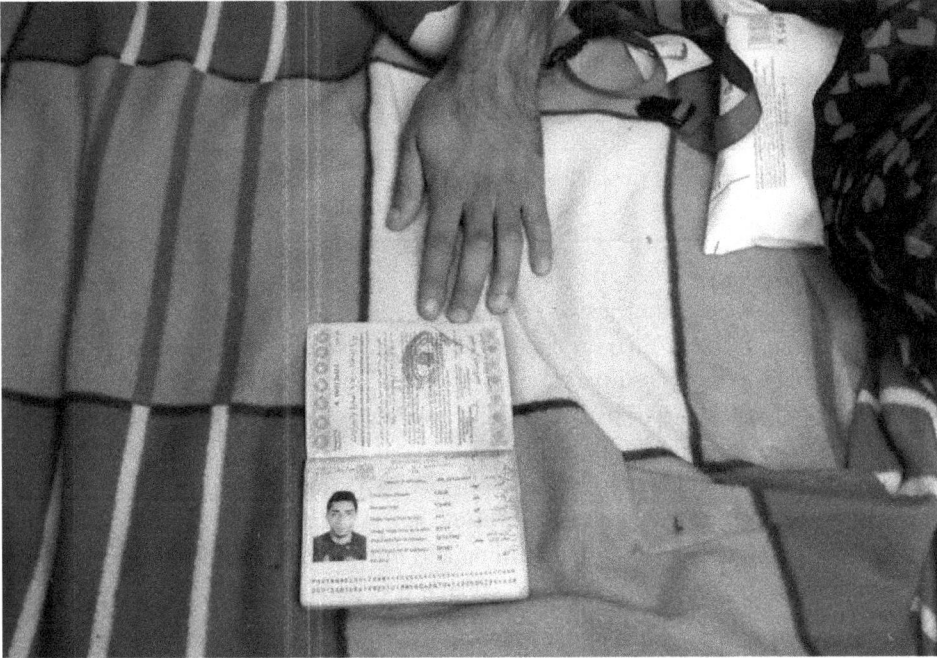

Ehab Ali Naser, a 23 year-old Syrian refugee, displays his Syrian passport in his tent at a makeshift camp on a street, in northern Paris, September 15, 2015. Ehab, in Paris for a month, arrived after an 18-month journey that started in his hometown of Homs, Syria, where he was a vendor at the souk. He spent a year in Lebanon, then traveled to Algeria and Morocco before he arrived in the Spanish port of Melila, and then headed to France. Currently he lives in a tent in a small refugee camp along a busy boulevard on the outskirts of Paris, September 15, 2015.

WASTE AND WORSE

Politicians indulge in remarkable hubris when they speak of fixing the root causes of migration crises. Other countries can do little in the short run to end many crises once they are underway. The root causes of the Hungarian upheaval lasted a generation. Military intervention by the West would likely have led to chaos and much greater human flight. Today's Middle East is no different. In a review of the entire history of refugee movements, the great political scientist Myron Weiner concluded that outside interventions can exacerbate and rarely halt mass departures from zones of conflict, particularly revolutions.

The lesson extends beyond sudden crises. Successful development assistance will typically increase emigration from low-income countries in the medium and long term. Officials commonly claim the opposite: that assisting economic development in poor countries, such as Yemen and Ethiopia, will reduce migration pressure from there in years to come. But research by one of us (Clemens) finds exactly the reverse pattern. Emigrants leave middle-income countries, such as Algeria and Albania, at about triple the rate that they leave the poorest countries. With greater earnings, they acquire the means, education, and contacts to depart. Only when countries surpass middle-income status, with further increases in prosperity at home, does migration pressure typically start to lessen.

What each rich country can do is alter what pulls people to that country specifically, once they have decided to flee their own land.

To be sure, donor-countries can sometimes affect push factors to some degree. They can reduce forced migration after natural disasters through humanitarian aid inside the origin country. And for those displaced by conflict, donors can provide emergency assistance to nearby countries, in today's case, Lebanon and Jordan, which are taking in the majority of migrants from Syria. Economists Ryan Bubb, Michael Kremer, and David Levine have proposed that rich countries could reduce onward flows by compensating third countries—elsewhere in the region or even far away—for the upfront costs of permanently resettling and integrating them. But in many crises, assistance in the original country of origin largely cannot deter departure.

A RACE TO THE BOTTOM

What each rich country can do is alter what pulls people to that country specifically, once they have decided to flee their own land. Germany has shown willingness to consider large numbers of asylum applications from Syria this year, possibly attracting more of those already in flight. Conversely, countries can deter entry with draconian physical barriers and tight rationing of asylum. Tony Abbott's Australia reduced unauthorized seaborne arrivals from about 20,000 in 2013 to almost zero in 2014, by instructing patrol ships to turn back migrant boats even if they appeared at risk of sinking.

These policies can effectively shunt migrants and asylum-seekers from one destination to another. But they create the pernicious incentive for other destination countries to do the same. If Slovakia and Hungary can divert fleeing Syrians to Germany, Slovakians and Hungarians can still free ride on the benefits of Germany's assistance: all share in the relief of watching fewer migrant deaths. But if numerous other countries follow suit, the stress on Germany can surge. This raises pressure for Germany to likewise try to divert migrants elsewhere.

Such a race-to-the-bottom does not deter desperate people from leaving places where hope has succumbed to violence and destitution. In surveys conducted by economist Linguère Mously Mbaye, half of irregular migrants from Senegal said that they would be undeterred by a 25 percent chance of death on their way to

Europe. So long as Europe is prosperous and free, the region as a whole will "pull" desperate people to its shores in times of crisis, despite roughly 20,000 deaths in the Mediterranean over the past decade.

The obvious solution is a cooperative mechanism to share responsibility for assistance.

Existing instruments of cooperation are terribly inadequate. The United Nations 1951 Convention Relating to the Status of Refugees enshrines the principle of "non-refoulement"—that people cannot be forcibly repatriated into persecution. But its obligations are national obligations, for the specific country in which a refugee arrives and seeks asylum. It only strengthens the incentives for each signatory to free-ride, physically diverting asylum seekers to transit countries and raising the standards of proof to grant asylum.

Asylum seekers and other crisis migrants can be apportioned by some more rational rule—rather than leaving cash-strapped southern Europe to cope with the crisis alone. This is the textbook solution to free-riding, and all participants can benefit. Coordination can serve each state's self-interest.

The current proposal for refugee quotas voted by the EU on September 22 is a step in this direction, but it is much too modest. It accepts the notion that this is a European problem rather than a global one. This has two consequences. First, the plan only addresses the needs of 120,000 refugees, although 400,000 already require resettlement from Syria alone. Second, it leaves refugee camps in the Middle East drastically underfunded, which is likely to produce more forced displacement next year. A broader global solution is needed to cope with the full scale of this crisis.

THE PAYOFF

The 1956 agreement that brought Andy Grove to America was built on this principle of cooperation for long-term self-interest. Austria was swamped with a flood of desperate Hungarians amounting to two percent of Hungary's population. By accepting a refugee influx equivalent to just 0.02 percent of the American population, the United States absorbed almost a quarter of the total flow out of Hungary. In so doing, it helped turn what could have been a burden into a benefit. It made assisting the Hungarians an investment with a positive return.

Syrian refugees disembark from a fishing boat at a beach on the Greek island of Lesbos after crossing a part of the Aegean Sea from the Turkish coast, September 27, 2015.

Countries struggle to absorb refugee flows when those flows are sudden and concentrated in a limited area. Their beds and other facilities are quickly swamped, and all they can do is build camps—usually hived off from the economy and life around them. This is what Lebanon and Jordan have been forced to do, with too little international assistance. Moreover, encamped people can give back little in economic terms, as the camp serving their immediate needs also isolates them from any contribution they could make.

But the problem is the encampment, not the refugees themselves. Indefinite camp life could have wasted Grove's talents; integration unleashed them. Refugees that can integrate and work generally perform well. Turkey's recent efforts to integrate Syrian arrivals have caused them to have a net positive effect on Turkish workers' wages, as economists Ximena del Carpio and Mathis Wagner have shown. Likewise refugees to the United States, after several years to get on their feet, economically outperform non-refugee migrants. Indeed, refugees in this country earn 20 percent more than other immigrants, work more hours, and speak better English, as economist Kalena Cortes has shown. They benefited the economy rather than burdening it.

Refugees to Europe likewise benefit the countries they go to, in the medium and long term. From 1994 to 2008, Denmark responded to successive international crises—in Yugoslavia and Somalia, and later in Iraq and Afghanistan—by admitting over 80,000 refugees, tripling the share of its population born outside the EU. Drawing on social security records covering all Danish workers, economists Mette Foged and Giovanni Peri have found that refugees raised the wages, employment, and occupational mobility of low-skill Danes. They did this by pushing Danes into more complex tasks and jobs, complementing many refugees' more basic skills.

People who flee crises are seeds, scattered by a storm.

These benefits are not automatic. They arise when migrant flows to any particular country are moderate. In major crises, this means that a coordinated group work to spread out the migrants and then integrate them. The United Nations High Commission for Refugees (UNHCR) estimates that the cost to host a Syrian refugee at Zaatari camp in Jordan can exceed $10,000 after a few years, without foreseeable economic benefits to UNHCR's donors. But Germany reaps tens to hundreds of thousands of dollars in lifetime added-value from each Syrian that is successfully integrated into its labor force, an incredible bargain for the one-off $14,000 per person resettlement cost. These benefits depend, however, on other countries' cooperation with Germany to mitigate the shock to the German system. And those other countries that cooperate can reap the same, positive long-term returns.

SEEDS, NOT SWARMS

We will make better policy when we think more pragmatically and less fearfully about what a migration crisis is. To many newspapers, migrants fleeing violence are a "flood," to extremists, they are an "invasion." To the British Prime Minister—in a comment he later withdrew—they are a "swarm."

History and reflection suggest a rather better metaphor: People who flee crises are seeds, scattered by a storm. When too many seeds are stuffed into one farm's soil, few germinate and everyone loses. If farmers fear this outcome enough, those fears can become self-fulfilling. As each farmer pushes the seeds downhill onto someone else's land, they pile up and become a burden. Alternatively, farmers can share the seeds and all reap a rich harvest.

These benefits are not immediate or automatic. But neither are they hypothetical. The world turned 200,000 desperate Hungarians into a gift. But only the world, not a country or two fulfilling its treaty obligations, could have done that: it took 37 nations working together. A global agreement with binding but equitable quotas could likewise resolve today's crisis—and beyond that, turn it from an act of generosity into a historic investment with worldwide payoff.

MICHAEL A. CLEMENS is a Senior Fellow at the Center for Global Development. JUSTIN SANDEFUR is a Senior Research Fellow at the Center for Global Development.

The Elephant in the Room

Islam and the Crisis of Liberal Values in Europe

Alexander Betts

Opponents of anti-immigration right-wing movement PEGIDA (Patriotic Europeans Against the Islamisation of the West) protest in Cologne, Germany, January 2016.

Europe is still struggling to cope with a massive influx of refugees, with over a million asylum seekers arriving across the Mediterranean Sea. Nearly all of them are Muslims. This fact has shaped public and political opinion but has rarely been openly and honestly discussed. Can a Europe of 28 member states share responsibility for a smaller number of refugees than is currently in Lebanon alone? Of course it can. In fact, most European countries need the labor.

The elephant in the room is an underlying Islamophobia. The simple fact is that European member states don't really want to welcome Muslim migrants. This has been explicit in the case of countries with vocal far-right parties and in central

European countries with Christian nationalist governments. But the liberal political elites of western Europe have steered clear of admitting that the biggest single barrier to coherent asylum and immigration policies is public anxiety about Islam. Far-right parties have pandered to these fears, stoking xenophobia. For the most part, though, people across the rest of the political spectrum have remained silent on the topic.

After all, the problem can't be that Europe believes it is unable to deal with the flow of migrants. It has historically been able to cope well with large influxes of refugees. Throughout the Cold War, for example, millions of people moved from eastern Europe to western Europe, fleeing communism. Europe then resettled hundreds of thousands of Vietnamese refugees in the 1980s and 1990s. It even took large numbers of migrants from Bosnia and Kosovo in the 1990s, including many Muslims—but this was before Islam became politically toxic. There has been far greater political skepticism toward those fleeing related conflicts in Afghanistan, Iraq, and now Syria.

More recently, the terrorist attack in Paris and reports of sexual assault and robbery in Cologne have been game changers for asylum in Europe. In Cologne, on New Year's Eve, more than 100 women and girls reported that gangs of men had assaulted them; authorities identified the attackers as North African or Arab men. Syrian refugees were immediately implicated. The backlash has been swift, and public opinion—even in relatively migrant-friendly Germany—has shifted away from refugees. Most countries have not gone as far as Slovakia, which has said it will welcome only Christian refugees, but there is an underlying fear of Islam guiding European policymaking.

Statistically, there is no greater likelihood that refugees will be involved in terrorism or crime than the general populations.

Broadly speaking, Europe's politicians have failed to articulate a vision for how its populations should think about Islam in Europe or to disentangle terms such as "refugees" and "migrants" from "terrorists" and "criminals." European responses have been muddled and hypocritical. Many countries have committed to deporting tens of thousands, even though they know this to be logistically impractical. Politicians have cowered from saying anything more specific about Islam and integration, for fear of electoral recrimination or media judgment. And policies have emerged across Europe that fundamentally contradict liberal values.

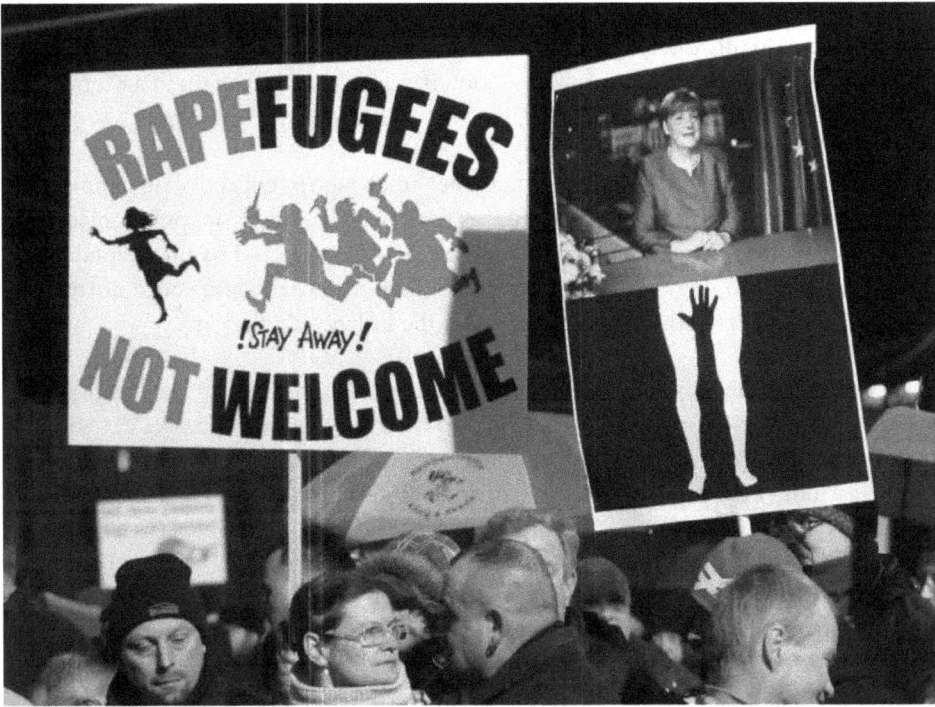

Members of LEGIDA, the Leipzig arm of the anti-Islam movement Patriotic Europeans Against the Islamisation of the West, take part in a rally in Leipzig, Germany, January 2016.

Statistically, there is no greater likelihood that refugees will be involved in terrorism or crime than the general populations. But perception matters. Germany's open immigration "experiment" is already under threat from a familiar pattern: a negative incident occurs that implicates refugees, the media pounces, the far right mobilizes, and the center-right shifts inches closer toward tightening borders.

Part of what makes this pattern so difficult to break is that centrist politics has declined in Europe. Centrist politicians have seen their vote share collapse; in the United Kingdom, for example, the dynamic between opposition leader Jeremy Corbyn and Conservative Prime Minister David Cameron resembles the polarized political atmosphere of the 1980s, when Margaret Thatcher was prime minister. The decline of the center has been shaped in part by its own failure to find persuasive answers on issues such as globalization, immigration, and integration. The left plays the rhetorical card of unconditional inclusion, and the right plays the rhetorical card of security.

The polarization of the debate has left a dearth of language through which remaining moderate politicians can articulate how Europeans should think about Islam, refugees, and migration. The starting point must be a clearheaded articulation and reassertion of liberal values.

Fundamentally, Europe is built on a shared belief in individual freedom. European values have thus historically included a commitment to human rights, democracy, gender equality, freedom of speech, freedom of religion, and the right to asylum. Most Europeans still believe in these values, but they are being poorly applied.

First, Europeans should avoid the tendency to engage in collective punishment. In Bornheim, Germany, all adult male refugees have been banned from public swimming pools after reports of sexual assault. This sort of policy should be unacceptable. Of course, people who migrate to Europe must adhere to its laws and social norms. But people should be judged—and punished—as the individuals they are.

Second, Europe should not waver in its commitment to freedom of religion. In a liberal community, people must be allowed to believe what they choose. Yet so many European policies are implicitly discriminatory; in Cardiff, the United Kingdom has forced asylum seekers to wear red wristbands at all times—a policy with harrowing historical parallels.

Third, Europe would have to do a better job upholding freedom of speech. The labeling of an idea as "religious" does not make it sacrosanct, beyond debate and criticism. Although hate speech crosses a threshold that requires regulation, "offense" on its own ought not to be criminalized. Charlie Hebdo's portrait of Aylan Kurdi, the three-year-old Syrian boy who drowned in the Mediterranean Sea, as a grown-up sexually lecherous man provoked outrage. But its intention was satirical: to mock those who believe that all Syrian refugees are sexually predatory. Moreover, politicians should resist the temptation to restrict freedom of speech on university campuses; in the United Kingdom, for example, a counterterrorist bill includes misguided measures allowing colleges to ban extremist speakers from coming to speak.

Europe's politicians have failed to articulate a vision for how its populations should think about Islam in Europe.

Finally, Europe must protect the right to asylum. European politicians must articulate clearly why refugees are a distinctive and privileged category of migrants. Germany has proposed to deport those immigrants convicted of crimes relating to Cologne. This is appropriate, with one exception: refugees should not be deported back to countries where they face persecution. European values dictate that whatever someone has done, nobody should ever be subjected to persecution, torture, or cruel, inhumane, and degrading treatment. Yet there is an increasingly open debate about deporting refugees, and European states have adopted stricter policies to deter asylum seekers, including Denmark's decision to deny refugees the right to property and to impose time limits on refugee family reunification.

The security threats that Europe faces are real. The self-proclaimed Islamic State (also known as ISIS) and other terrorist groups threaten lives and values. Many of the refugees coming to Europe are themselves fleeing ISIS-related violence. The way to address security challenges is through better intelligence and criminal justice, not through restrictions on the right to asylum. The United Kingdom has avoided a mainland terrorist attack over the past decade because of its superior intelligence services, not because of its immigration policies. Bolstering those services, rather than undermining liberal values, is the best response to terror.

INA FASSBENDER / REUTERS

Riot police stand in front of supporters of anti-immigration right-wing movement PEGIDA during a rally in Cologne, Germany, January 2016.

The last difficult question that Europeans might ask is: Is Islam compatible with liberal values? Generally, yes. In formulating policy, European leaders would be wise not to see Islam as incompatible with liberalism but to work with religious leaders to ensure that it isn't.

Questions of migration management and integration policy are valid social concerns, but they must be addressed through informed and rational debate. Against a backdrop of incoherent and muddled thinking, Europe needs a new centrist politics. It must be grounded in liberalism, transcending both the xenophobia of the far right and the moral relativism of the far left. The center's strength depends on its ability to show practical ways to navigate Europe's emerging politics of fear. Only then will

Europe be able to openly and honestly grapple with how to engage with refugees and migration in a changing world.

ALEXANDER BETTS is Professor of Forced Migration and International Affairs at the University of Oxford, where he is also Director of the Refugee Studies Centre. Follow him on Twitter @alexander_betts.

© Foreign Affairs

Jordan's Refugee Experiment

A New Model for Helping the Displaced

Alexander Betts and Paul Collier

MUHAMMAD HAMED / REUTERS

Syrian children decorate a wall at their school in Jordan's Zaatari refugee camp, March 2014.

The Syrian refugee crisis has attracted Western attention largely because of its modest spillover into Europe. But this spillover represents a mere fraction of the misery caused by mass displacement today: only around 15 percent of Syria's 5.8 million refugees have attempted to reach Europe, and the Syrian refugee surge is itself only one of several around the world.

The challenge of mass displacement is largely one of geographical concentration: nearly 60 percent of the world's refugees are hosted by just ten haven countries, each bordering a conflict zone. It is in these countries—Jordan, Lebanon, and Turkey, in the case of the Syrian civil war—where new approaches are most direly needed: policies that are sustainable and scalable and that allow displaced people to learn, work, and flourish until they are able to return to their homes and rebuild their societies. With European leaders focused on keeping Syrian refugees out of the continent, such policies have so far been lacking.

It is tempting to suggest that refugees become temporary citizens in host countries, with access to education, work, and other rights for the length of their stays. But with few exceptions, such as Uganda, host countries that neighbor conflicts are generally unwilling to open their labor markets to refugees, let alone integrate them socially or politically. In countries where this is the case, what kind of alternatives might be available?

By reducing the need to repeatedly mobilize for emergency responses, SEZs would help policymakers focus on providing higher-quality assistance.

In October, Foreign Affairs published our proposal for a new approach to the Syrian refugee crisis. By allowing displaced Syrians to work in special economic zones (SEZs) in Jordan, we argued, Amman could provide displaced Syrians with the jobs, education, and autonomy they need while advancing its own industrial development. We focused on the King Hussein Bin Talal Development Area (KHBTDA), an SEZ into which the Jordanian government has already invested more than 100 million dollars in infrastructure and which lies a short distance from the Zaatari refugee camp, which houses some 83,000 refugees. By allowing Syrian refugees to work and receive training in the KHBTDA alongside Jordanian nationals, we suggested, the Jordanian government could transform refugees from a burden into an advantage, all the while preserving their autonomy and incubating a Syrian economy in exile in preparation for the civil war's eventual end.

Since our article was published, our idea has gained political traction. Over the course of the winter, Jordanian King Abdullah, British Prime Minister David Cameron, and World Bank President Jim Yong Kim developed the idea into a full-fledged proposal, formally launching it at the London Conference on Syria in February 2016. A pilot program that will grant some 150,000 refugees the right to work will likely begin in Jordan this summer.

TIME FOR A CHANGE

A fresh approach to mass displacement is needed now more than ever. Since April 2015, when waves of refugees started arriving on European shores, the responses offered by EU states have been ever-worsening failures. Not only are the politics behind the European response to the refugee crisis dysfunctional, the policies they have produced have neglected the West's obligations to come to the aid of the displaced.

Consider the recent deal negotiated by German Chancellor Angela Merkel and Turkish President Recep Tayyip Erdogan, which aims to reduce the number of migrants making the dangerous trip across the Aegean from Turkey to Greece. Under the deal, the European Union has promised to give Turkey some six billion euros and assured Ankara that it will speed up the talks surrounding the country's accession to the European Union, granting Turkish citizens the right to visa-free travel in the European Union in the meantime. In return, Turkey has agreed to a "one-in-one out" policy, under which European governments will return nearly all the migrants and refugees who arrive in Greece to Turkish soil; Turkey will then send an equal number of Syrian refugees, but no more than 73,000, directly to Europe.

STEFAN ROUSSEAU / POOL / REUTERS

Jordanian King Abdullah at a conference on the humanitarian crisis in Syria, in London, February 2016.

The logic of the deal, in the words of David Cameron, is "to break the link between getting on a boat and getting settlement in Europe." But for a number of reasons, the pact is already unraveling.

It has always been unclear, for one, whether Greece has the capacity to forcefully deport thousands of refugees and migrants to Turkey. Turkey, for its part, lacks the asylum system needed to effectively protect non-Syrian asylum seekers, as it is obligated under the deal, and reports from Human Rights Watch suggest that Turkish authorities are already returning non-Syrian refugees, including some Afghans, to danger in their countries of origin. Nor is this all. EU countries have not yet committed the necessary resettlement places for Syrians coming out of Turkey; European authorities, fearful of backlash against violations of human rights committed under a plan that UN agencies have opposed, will probably drag their feet on the deportations to avoid bad press; and given Turkey's authoritarian drift, the European Union will probably struggle to fast track Ankara's push for membership anyway. But perhaps most disconcerting is the fact that the deal was born of fear and hatred, not of a recognition of the West's moral obligations. The result is a coercive, exclusionary policy that will do little to help the dispossessed.

Perhaps because it has sensed the need for a more comprehensive approach, the European Commission has announced a new initiative: one that would transform the European Asylum Support Office from an advisory body into a regulatory entity, setting pan-European asylum rules and requiring countries to take quotas of refugees. Apart from the fact that the treaty change required to enact such a policy is probably impossible in the European Union's current political climate, the fact that the European Commission's response to its failures so far is to suggest further centralizing its power shows that it has misdiagnosed the problem.

A pilot program that will grant some 150,000 refugees the right to work will likely begin in Jordan this summer.

If Europe really wants to help displaced Syrians, it should start by helping to provide opportunities for employment and education in the host countries bordering Syria. The governments of those countries should not have to threaten to expel refugees to Europe in order to attract European support: instead, the European Commission should set rules that distribute the financial burden of such assistance among EU countries. The European Union needs to encourage European firms to bring jobs to development zones in the host countries so that refugees can restore their autonomy by earning a living. And the European Commission needs to reform the European Union's market access rules so that goods produced by refugees can be sold in Europe without impediment. Once such policies are in place, the need to reach pan-European agreement on migration and refugee policies, which should be only a minor component of Europe's approach to mass displacement, will be more manageable.

ZONAL DEVELOPMENT'S NEXT STEP

We first developed the idea that special economic zones could offer employment opportunities for Syrian refugees during a visit to refugee camps and urban areas in Jordan in April 2015 (our trip was supported by the WANA Institute, a Jordanian think tank). As we developed our essay for Foreign Affairs, the Jordanian government prepared an internal white paper that reflected and developed the approach.

Abdullah introduced the plan to Cameron in September, during the British prime minister's visit to Jordan and Lebanon. Over the following months, the UK government convened a series of technical discussions with the Jordanian government and within its own Department for International Development, exploring, among other issues, the possibilities that the World Bank might finance infrastructure projects in the SEZs and that the European Union might grant trade concessions to the exports produced there. At the World Economic Forum in January, Queen Rania of Jordan promoted the idea and a number of manufacturing company CEOs began to express interest.

The formal launch of the pilot project came the next month, at the London conference on Syrian refugees on February 4. Both Abdullah and Cameron spoke about the pilot, as did a number of business leaders, among them Andy Clarke, the CEO of Asda, the UK subsidiary of Wal-Mart. Cameron argued in his opening remarks that, in addition to the $11 billion in aid that governments pledged at the conference, the meeting's "mold-breaking" contribution would be the investment it secured in jobs and development in host countries neighboring Syria. The idea drew widespread support: Former British Prime Minister Gordon Brown, for instance, wrote that "economic zones should be created in Lebanon, Jordan, and Turkey" in an op-ed published in The Guardian on the day of the conference. A number of governments agreed to provide Jordan with around $2 billion in assistance and investment, in return for which Jordan would grant 150,000 work permits to Syrian refugees. Those Syrians would find jobs alongside Jordanian nationals in five SEZs Amman planned to improve, building on existing development areas such as the KHBTA.

ALKIS KONSTANTINIDIS / REUTERS

A Syrian refugee family gathers around a bonfire next to the Greek-Macedonian border fence, at a makeshift camp near Idomeni, Greece, March 2016.

We are confident that pilot programs will begin in the summer of 2016. But a number of uncertainties remain. First, there is not yet a consensus within the Jordanian government on the number of work permits that the country will provide for the pilot programs (an initial figure of 150,000 has been suggested) and the portion of those that will be reserved for Jordanian nationals. (The extent of Jordan's enthusiasm for the project may depend on the willingness of European firms to demonstrate their own interest in it.) Next, questions remain about the extent to which funds pledged by donors will support public-sector jobs instead of private-sector employment in the SEZs. The project still needs to secure EU trade concessions, an end toward which its organizers are now making progress, and it needs to attract more interest from manufacturing companies, although Asda and Ikea, for example, have offered some initial support. Some major European states have yet to put serious effort into encouraging firms to play a role: the German government, for instance, has been preoccupied with the refugees who are already in Germany. Finally, the extent to which the World Bank will be able to invest in infrastructural development related to the pilot programs remains unclear.

These uncertainties aside, the pilot now seems likely to go ahead. Once that happens, the world must pay close attention to its strengths and weaknesses—both to ensure the success of the program in Jordan and to consider how the model of zonal development employed there might be applied to the other countries hosting refugees.

That won't be as simple as rolling out the model used in Jordan elsewhere. In some countries, such as Uganda, where refugees have a number of socioeconomic freedoms, refugees may be able to gradually gain rights to employment and political participation equivalent to those of citizens. In countries that resist the full participation of refugees in their economies and societies, incubation, rather than integration, could be the focus: refugees, along with their jobs, could be relocated to their countries of origin after the end of the conflicts that have displaced them. Nor need all such programs involve manufacturing, as Jordan's will: the logic of zonal development could also be applied to economies that seek to develop other sectors. No matter which industries they support, however, SEZs can permanently offer infrastructure to assist the displaced in countries that repeatedly take in large numbers of refugees, as so many haven countries do. By reducing the need to repeatedly mobilize for emergency responses, SEZs would help policymakers focus on providing higher-quality assistance.

The purpose of refugee protection should be to provide people with rights and opportunities until they can go home or integrate into their host societies. States need to fulfill this mission in a way that benefits host societies even as it promotes human flourishing. The key to doing so is to shift from a purely humanitarian approach to a development approach, with jobs and education at the center.

ALEXANDER BETTS is Professor of Forced Migration and International Affairs and Director of the Refugee Studies Centre at the University of Oxford. He is the author of *Survival Migration: Failed Governance and the Crisis of Displacement*. Follow him on Twitter @alexander_betts.   PAUL COLLIER is Professor of Economics and Public Policy at the Blavatnik School of Government at the University of Oxford. He is the author of *Exodus: How Migration Is Changing Our World*.

France on Fire

The Charlie Hebdo Attack and the Future of al Qaeda

Jytte Klausen

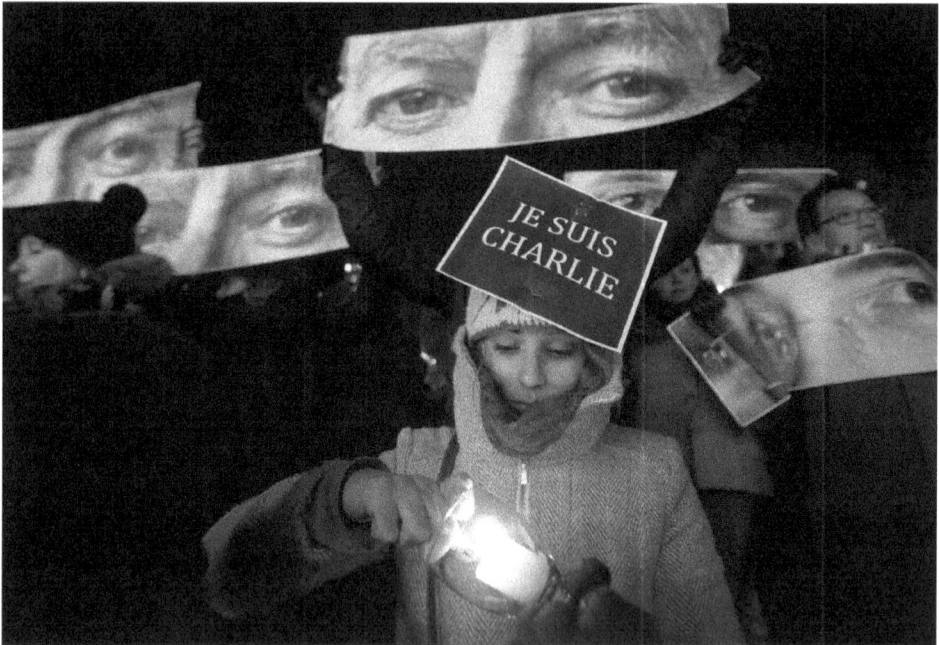

A vigil in New York, January 7, 2015.

Early on January 7, masked gunmen stormed the editorial office of the French satirical magazine Charlie Hebdo and killed 12 people. The death toll may still rise. The attack coincided with an editorial meeting at the paper, with key staffers assembled. According to eyewitness reports, the perpetrators forced their way into a back office, calling out the names of the editor and cartoonists before shooting them. The assassins, presumed to be al Qaeda members, escaped.

The death toll makes this week's attack the most significant on French soil since the Nazi occupation—a huge milestone in al Qaeda's campaign against the West. It is part of a long line of plots to kill media figures for their symbolic value in the West as paragons of free speech and to some Muslims as examples of the evil of secularism. For the terrorists, the staff of Hebdo were particularly appealing targets, since it was one of the few European papers that, in the wake of the 2009 Danish cartoon episode, continued to publish irascible cartoons of Muhammad, ridiculing the pieties of extremist Islamists. In fact, the paper's editorial office had already been firebombed in 2011, after it published a special "Muhammad issue" ostensibly featuring the Muslim Prophet as guest editor. Ongoing threats to the paper were public and well-known.

The French line on the attack is that it was a unique incident carried out by professional terrorists, assumed to have learned their skills in Syria. The three men identified by the French police as the gunmen are the stuff of French nightmares. All three spoke in French, and, exiting the scene of their crime, they told bystanders to tell the media that they came from al Qaeda in the Arabian Peninsula (AQAP). One member of the cell, Hamyd Mourad, is just 18 and is said to have attended high school in the northern city of Reims. The other two are brothers—Said Kouachi, who is 34, and Cherif Kouachi, who is 32. The Kouachi brothers would have been well-known to the French police. Cherif was arrested in January 2005 and convicted three years later in connection with a recruitment ring that planned to send French residents to fight for al Qaeda in Iraq. At the time, Cherif thanked the police for preventing him from going to Iraq, but his regrets may not have been sincere. In May 2010, he was arrested again in connection with a plot to free two well-known French-Algerian jihadists, Djamel Beghal and Smain Ait Ali Belkacem, the perpetrators of the 1995 Paris Métro bombings.

It is not necessarily contradictory to say that the attackers were from AQAP and that they had picked up their skills in Syria, where most fighters are presumed to be allied with the Islamic State of Iraq and al-Sham (ISIS) or smaller al Qaeda–affiliated groups. The Yemen-based AQAP is known to have sent fighters to Syria. And al Qaeda, facing competitive pressure from ISIS, was surely desperate for a victory. It is therefore reasonable to assume that the killings in France could be an attempt to remind the world that al Qaeda is still relevant.

Indeed, some commentators had predicted just such an outcome and had even gone so far as to say that al Qaeda faced sure decline with ISIS on the scene. But the U.S. government was never keen to discount the al Qaeda threat. And the reality is that the rise of one organization is not tantamount to the decline of the other. Rather, today there are simply far more trained killers, from more groups, on the loose in western Europe than at any previous time in al Qaeda's 20-year history of menacing the West.

This particular attack fits well within the old al Qaeda playbook. The organization, specifically AQAP, has made the assassination of cartoonists its special beat. In 2011, the senior al Qaeda figure Anwar al-Awlaki issued an online sermon titled "The Dust Will Never Settle Down," telling his adherents to take matters in their own hands and kill cartoonists who offended the Prophet. The video has been linked to a large number of attacks and threats against Western individuals perceived to have defamed the Prophet. In March 2013, Inspire, the online magazine published by AQAP, featured a Wanted poster listing the enemies of the Prophet. Hebdo's editor in chief, Stéphane Charbonnier, was on the list. He was among those killed on Wednesday.

Even the template for the Hebdo attack was nauseatingly familiar. Emerging details suggest that the assassins might have had inside information about the operations and layout of Hebdo's office, which they used to know exactly where to show up and when. That sort of detailed preparation is the hallmark of an al Qaeda–directed operation, as opposed to "homegrown" attacks that often fail because of the incompetence of the plotters. In 2009 and 2010, authorities foiled similar plots to storm the editorial offices of Jyllands-Posten, the Danish newspaper responsible for originally publishing the controversial cartoons of Muhammad. David Coleman Headley (born Daood Sayed Gilani), a Chicago-based American citizen who also conducted advance scouting for the 2008 Mumbai attacks, traveled twice to Denmark to help plan the Jyllands-Posten plot. A second attempt to attack the newspaper was made in December 2010. In this case, the assassins were Swedish residents who had been under surveillance for some time.

The difference today is the skill with which the attacks were carried out. France has seen a number of such incidents perpetrated by individuals who have left the country to fight abroad and then returned home to apply their skills on domestic "soft" targets.

For example, Mohammed Merah, a 23-year-old man from Toulouse whose family has deep roots in the French extremist milieu, targeted French soldiers of Muslim origin and a Jewish school in a series of killings in March 2012. Reminiscent of this week's attack, Merah's attacks were executed with precision and skill. He filmed them, intending to post the videos online. (French authorities prevented this from happening.) Mehdi Nemmouche, also a French veteran from the insurgency in Syria, carried out a precise attack on pedestrians at a Jewish museum in May last year. He, too, filmed the attack for later distribution. The Hebdo shooters apparently did not film themselves, and online jihadists quickly took to Twitter, bemoaning the absence of footage. They need not worry. Bystanders using their cell phones to film and post videos have already flooded social media.

This week, the war with the jihadists ratcheted up. And much of the media reacted in fear. The Associated Press quickly removed all content from its website featuring pictures of Hebdo's pages. It is safe to expect the managers and owners of other publishing companies and the news media to follow suit. But that is the wrong reaction. Al Qaeda, ISIS, and any number of other groups continue their war against the West, but there is not a trained team of assassins from al Qaeda lurking in every parking lot. The French are right. It was a unique attack. The proper response to the challenge of transnational terrorism is to increase domestic security and information sharing among governments about citizens traveling to Syria and Iraq. Europe's open borders require a security infrastructure to match.

JYTTE KLAUSEN is Lawrence A. Wien Professor of International Cooperation at Brandeis University.

Laïcité Without Égalité

Can France Be Multicultural?

Jonathan Laurence

Blue, white, and red candles at the Place de la Republique in Paris, France, November 16, 2015.

"Imagine" by John Lennon has become the impromptu French anthem after a pianist's moving performance in front of the blood-soaked Bataclan concert hall the morning following last week's attack in Paris. It is not hard to hear strains of "La Marseillaise" in this secular prayer for "a brotherhood of man." But beyond such fraternité, Lennon also imagines a world without religion, and that is something few French agree on.

French Christians, Muslims, Jews, and others are as angered as everyone else by the "holy war" being waged by the self-proclaimed Islamic State (also known as ISIS). But they do not necessarily subscribe to the idea of a post-religious society, as France sometimes appears to be, any more than they embraced Charlie Hebdo's brand of satire.

They heard "Je suis Charlie" not as a defense of press freedom or a right to offend, but as a barb directed at them. On Sunday, a former senior government official gave a scathing interview demanding that Muslim representatives stop "shirking responsibility."

In his historic address to a joint session of Parliament on November 16, French President François Hollande sought to calm domestic tensions. He singled out jihad and ISIS but made no reference to Islam or Muslims. "It hurts to say it, but we know that these were French people who killed other French people." Hollande added that the terrorists are "individuals who start out by committing crimes, [then] become radicalized." In other words, he emphasized, violating French law was the first stop on the terrorists' slide to violent extremism—not the fact of their having been born into a given religious community. The high percentage of French converts to Islam among the recruits to ISIS—20 percent overall and 25 percent of all female ISIS recruits—testifies to this point.

Reactions to the speech have emphasized Hollande's martial tone and the lack of a long-term strategy to rid secular France of violent religious extremism. One secular intellectual concluded in Sunday's Le Figaro that "laïcité is unintelligible and even shocking" for practicing Muslims, who view it as "an injunction to abandon their religion."

A woman wears a tape with the word 'Liberte' (Freedom) on her mouth during a silent protest for the victims of the shooting at the Paris offices of weekly newspaper Charlie Hebdo, at the Pariser Platz square in Berlin, January 11, 2015.

Laïcité was a revolutionary secularism that was hostile to any intermediary associations, especially religious ties, between citizens and the state. A recent book by Jean Baubérot catalogs no fewer than seven different styles of laïcité in the last two centuries. The state has sometimes been anti-religious and sometimes dirigiste—that is, interested in directing religious practice. Today's laïcité is "identity based," Baubérot argues, and it is theoretically supportive of religious life that eschews the public or political sphere. For example, the state assumes most of the costs for thousands of religious schools. For historical reasons these are mostly Catholic, but there are hundreds of Jewish schools, too. Expanding this right to include Muslim schools is a natural step that would enhance, rather than diminish, as the Le Figaro author might contend, French laïcité.

The last census to even indicate respondents' religion was conducted in 1872.

But since the late 1990s, governments have had a hard time making such changes out of a well-grounded fear of the far right. The National Front has haunted French politics during the same 40-year period that a native-born Muslim minority has come of age. It's no coincidence that a law banning headscarves in French public schools came on the heels of the right-wing politician Jean-Marie Le Pen's best electoral performance in April 2002. That law had the ironic consequence of creating demand for private Muslim schools for families desiring a religious education—that is, it disintegrated rather than integrated Muslims. Qualifying for state support for schools is a long process that only a handful of Muslim institutions have mastered to date. The problems go beyond schooling. The last census to even indicate respondents' religion was conducted in 1872, and a 1978 law (later softened) prohibited official record keeping on ethnicity and race. Affirmative action has always been unpopular because it violates the principles of equality and colorblindness. And ethnic or religious lobbies are viewed with suspicion.

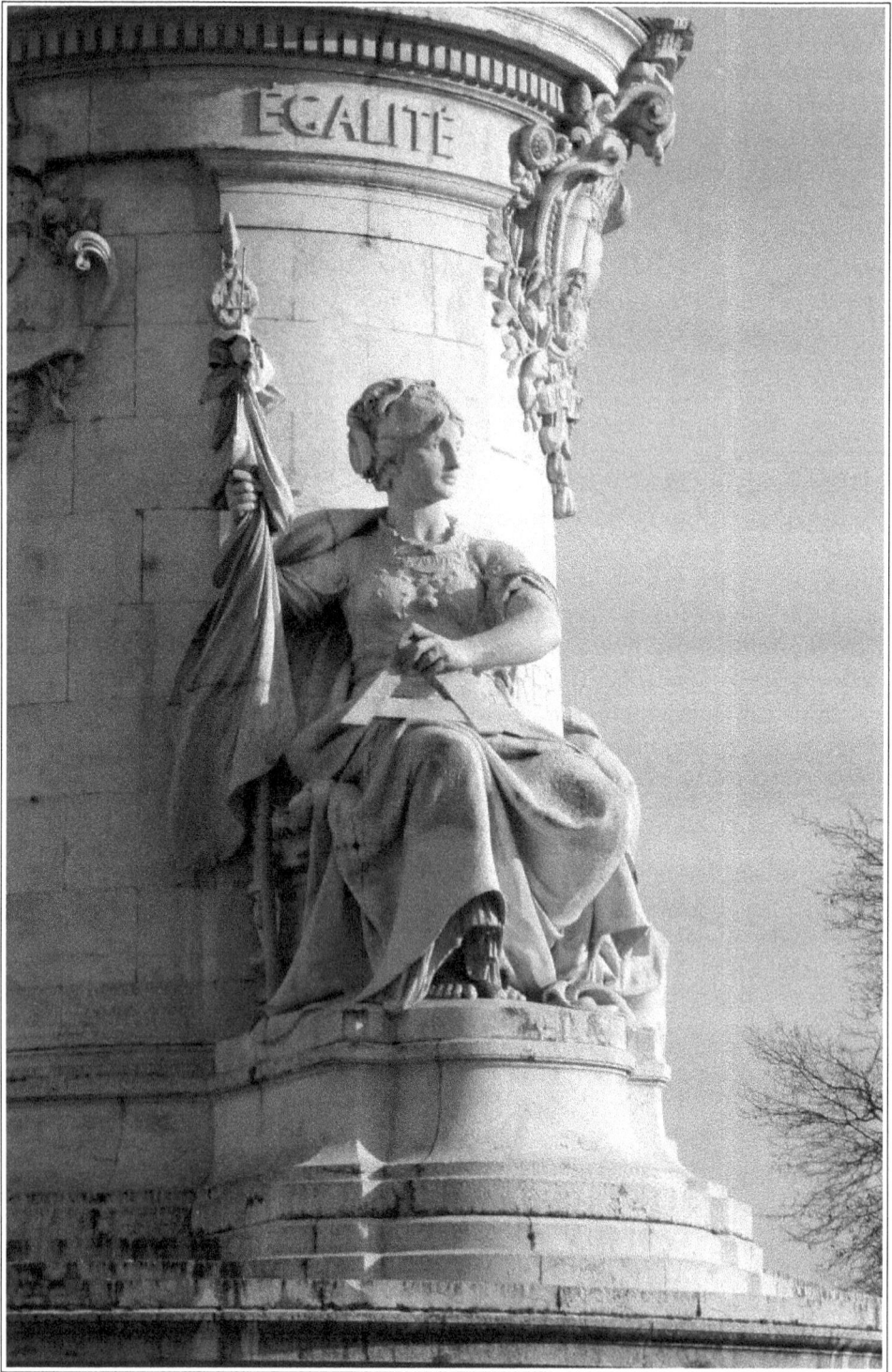

Monument at the place de la Republique, Paris.

Policymakers and the public have thus been left guessing about everything from the exact size of the new Muslim minority to their performance in schools and on the job market—just as the second and third generations emerged on the scene. In a sense, France's official ignorance about its citizens' race and religion is a laudable virtue dating back to the abolition of feudalism in 1789. It holds the promise of emancipation from one's origins.

But statistically dissolving the children and grandchildren of immigrants into the general citizenry also reflects wishful thinking that integration can simply be decreed. This approach hampered the study of the new generations' socioeconomic experiences and the creation of appropriate policy responses to the difficulties they encountered. Radicalization is indeed a French problem, not just a Muslim one. But if there is only a single unitary peuple français, in Hollande's words, then there are no communities that are marginalized, no communities from which to draw necessary strength and resources.

Concessions to organized religion have never sat well with a wide cross section of French political elites.

French demographers have recently begun to measure the trajectories of immigrant-origin citizens, but the notion of "ethnic statistics" still raises hackles. Political integration has also come along at a very deliberate speed—at the national level, there have been a handful of ministerial appointments of minorities. French Muslims are assumed to make up around eight percent of the national population, but there is only one first-term "Muslim" MP, who is the child of North African labor migrants and happens not to be very religious. French authorities have also adapted in other ways. At critical junctures over the last two centuries, French governments have gradually liberalized France's state-church policy to extend accords guaranteeing religious freedoms—including de facto state support for prayer spaces and religious education—to the Jewish Consistoire, Catholic Church, and Protestant Federation. In 2003, the French Council of the Muslim Faith (CFCM) joined in. Such overt political contact with religious leadership remains controversial: concessions to organized religion have never sat well with a wide cross section of French political elites.

Also somewhat controversial were the government's consultations with Muslim civil society groups after Charlie Hebdo. These looked beyond mosque administrators to include dozens of individual Muslim citizens with leadership potential. The resulting instance de dialogue has only an advisory role and meets but once or twice annually. It is not meant to replace the CFCM, but around half of its members come from the same pool of religious associations as the council. January's attacks also pushed the government to introduce reforms to make chaplains more available in prisons, to require the certification of imams who will preach in French mosques, and to move to establish Islamic theology faculties where those for Christianity and Judaism already exist.

This time around, the government seems to be focused on what has come to be seen as necessary repression: closing radical mosques, arresting known radicals, and prosecuting the war on ISIS in Syria. Representatives of Muslim civil society organizations—religious and secular—will bear more pressure to prove that they are part of the solution. The CFCM is preparing a call for national unity to be read aloud in France's 2,500 Islamic prayer spaces on the first Friday after the November attacks. The country's largest Muslim student group published an emotional video of condolences and condemnation that has been warmly welcomed to the national discussion.

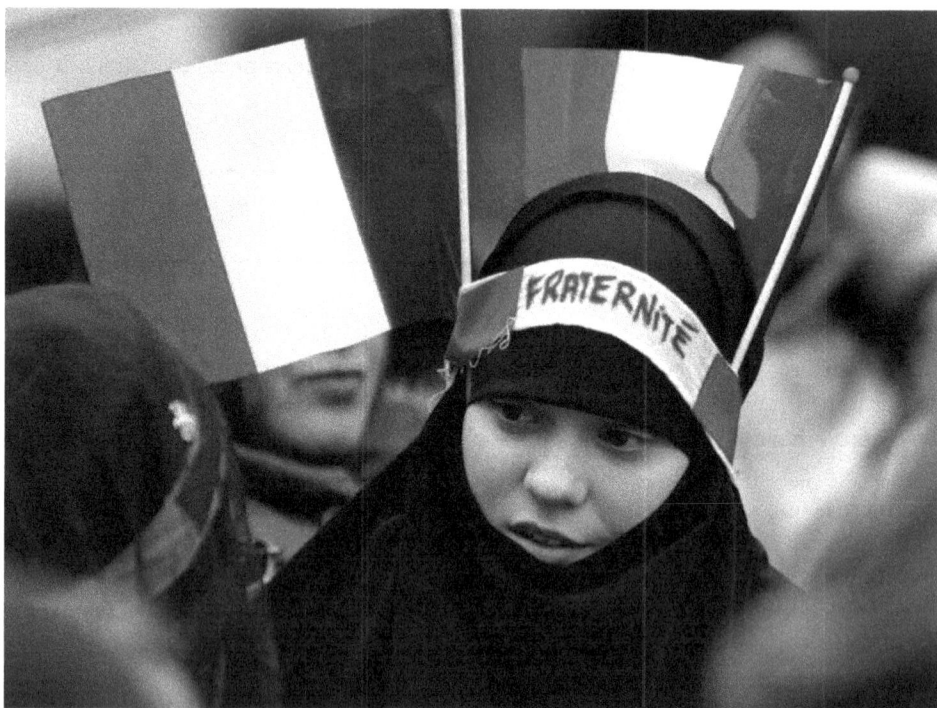

CHARLES PLATIAU / REUTERS

A girl marches among about 3,000 Sikhs from across Europe to protest a French ban on religious symbols in state schools, January 31, 2004.

This stands in contrast to the spirit of fraternité that pervaded in January after the Charlie Hebdo attacks. In response to the killing of 12 people who were targeted for their membership in small communities—journalists, Jews, and police officers—nearly four million joined marches across France on January 11. With the simple messages of their printed signs—Je suis Charlie, Je suis juif, Je suis flic (I am Charlie, I am Jewish, I am a cop)—demonstrators formed a symbolic human shield around the attack's targets. That is the positive side of French citizenship, rooted in a fundamental belief that everyone is the same.

Equality was the assessment of the terrorists, too, who killed indiscriminately on Friday. But it is also incorrect and gives an incomplete portrait of a complex society. Until French policymakers find a way to give all citizens equal rights to communal attachments, France will not be able to find a way to bring them fully together.

JONATHAN LAURENCE is Associate Professor of Political Science at Boston College and Nonresident Senior Fellow in Foreign Policy studies at the Brookings Institution. He is the author of *The Emancipation of Europe's Muslims* and *Integrating Islam: Political and Religious Challenges in Contemporary France* (with Justin Vaisse).

Europe's Dangerous Multiculturalism

Why the Continent Fails Minority Groups

Kenan Malik

Members of the movement of Patriotic Europeans Against the Islamisation of the West (PEGIDA) hold flags during a demonstration march in Dresden, January 25, 2015. The text on the placard reads "Stop multiculture. My homeland remains German!"

What is it that draws thousands of young Europeans to jihadism and violence? What is it that has led 4,000 to travel to Syria to fight for the so-called Islamic State (ISIS)? And what is it that leads European citizens to engage in barbarous carnage such as those witnessed last month in Paris?

The conventional answer is that they have become "radicalized," a process through which vulnerable Muslims are groomed for extremist violence by those who champion hate. The radicalization argument consists of four broad elements. The first is the claim that people become terrorists because they acquire certain, usually religiously informed, extremist ideas. The second is that these ideas are acquired in a different way from that in which people acquire other extremist or oppositional ideas. The third is that there is a conveyor belt that leads from grievance to religiosity to the adoption of radical beliefs to terrorism. And the fourth is the insistence that what makes people vulnerable to acquiring such ideas is that they are poorly integrated into society.

The trouble is that these assumptions, which underlie much of Europe's domestic counterterrorism policy, are wrong. Many studies show, for instance, that those who are drawn to jihadist groups are not necessarily attracted by fundamentalist religious ideas. A 2008 study by Britain's MI5 on extremism that was leaked to the press observed that "far from being religious zealots, a large number of those involved in terrorism do not practice their faith regularly."

There is also little evidence that jihadists acquire their ideas differently from other kinds of groups, even though conventional wisdom suggests that their ideology comes from hate preachers and the like, whereas other radical ideas are born of different circumstances. Jamie Bartlett, head of the Violence and Extremism program at the British think tank Demos, argues that such terrorism "shares much in common with other counter-cultural, subversive groups of predominantly angry young men."

Nor is there any evidence of a straight path leading people from radical ideas to jihadist violence. A 2010 British government report concluded that the conveyor belt thesis "seems to both misread the radicalization process and to give undue weight to ideological factors."

And finally, there is much evidence that those who join jihadi groups are anything but poorly integrated, at least in the conventional sense of integration. A survey of British jihadists by researchers at Queen Mary College in London found that support for jihadism is unrelated to social inequality or poor education; rather, those drawn to jihadist groups were 18-to 20-year-olds from wealthy families who spoke English at home and were educated to a high, often university, level. In fact, "youth, wealth, and being in education," as the study put it, "were risk factors."

In a sense, the radicalization argument looks at the jihadists' journey from back to front. It begins with the jihadists as they are at the end of their journey—enraged about the West, and with a black-and-white view of Islam—and assumes that these are the reasons they have come to be as they are. What draws young people (and the majority of would-be jihadis are in their teens or twenties) to jihadi violence is a search for something a lot less definable: for identity, for meaning, for belongingness, for respect. Insofar as they are alienated, it is not because wannabe jihadis are poorly integrated, in the sense of not speaking the local language or being unaware of local customs or having little interaction with others in the society. Theirs is a much more existential form of alienation.

A young Muslim girl has two French flags and a headband which reads "Fraternity" on her headscarf as she march among about 3,000 Sikhs from across Europe protesting on a Paris boulevard to defend their traditional headgear against a looming French ban on religious symbols in state schools, January 31, 2004.

ANGSTY

There is, of course, nothing new in expressions of alienation and angst. The youthful search for identity and meaning is cliché. What is different today is the social context in which such alienation and searching occurs. We live in an age of growing social disintegration, in which many people feel peculiarly disengaged from mainstream social institutions.

The real starting point for the making of a homegrown jihadist is not radicalization but this kind of social disconnection, a sense of estrangement from, resentment of, Western society. It is because they have already rejected mainstream culture, ideas, and norms that some Muslims search for an alternative vision of the world. It is not surprising that many wannabe jihadis are either converts to Islam, or Muslims who discovered their faith only relatively late. In both cases, disenchantment with what else is on offer has led them to the black-and-white moral code of extremist Islamism. It is not, in other words, a question of being "groomed" or "indoctrinated" but of losing faith in mainstream moral frameworks and searching for an alternative.

In the past, disaffection with the mainstream may have led people, certainly in Europe, to join movements for political change, from far-left groups to labor movement organizations to anti-racist campaigns.

Disengagement is, of course, not simply a Muslim issue. There is today widespread disenchantment with the political process, a sense of being politically voiceless, a despair that neither mainstream political parties nor social institutions such as the church or trade unions seem to comprehend their concerns and needs.

All this has inevitably shaped how young people, and not just those of Muslim backgrounds, experience their alienation, and how they are able to act upon it. In the past, such disaffection with the mainstream may have led people, certainly in Europe, to join movements for political change, from far-left groups to labor movement organizations to anti-racist campaigns. Such organizations gave idealism and social grievance a political form, and a mechanism for turning disaffection into social change.

Today, such campaigns and organizations can seem as out-of-touch as mainstream institutions. In part, this is because the broad ideological divides that had characterized politics for much of the past two hundred years have been all but erased. Distinctions between left and right have become less meaningful. The weakening of labor organizations and other institutions, the decline of collectivist ideologies, the expansion of the market into many nooks and crannies of life—all have helped create a more socially, fragmented society.

MICHAEL DALDER / REUTERS

A member of BAGIDA, the Bavarian section of the anti-immigration movement Patriotic Europeans Against the Islamisation of the West (PEGIDA), holds a poster depicting German Chancellor Angela Merkel during a march in the center of Munich, January 19, 2015. The text reads 'Mommy multicultural. Merkel's migration policy.'

In turn, identity politics has become more salient; fragmentation has encouraged people to define themselves in increasingly narrow ethnic or cultural terms. Public policies aimed at integrating minorities have only helped exacerbate this process. After the Paris attacks, many commentators insisted that at least part of the blame must lie with French "assimilationist" social policies which, they claimed, had failed to integrate Muslims and had created a more divided society. Social policies that took more account of the diversity of French society, they suggested, would have better served France.

Others responded that it made little sense to blame French social policies. Belgium, and in particular the Brussels area of Molenbeek, has become a nursery for jihadists even though Belgian social policy is more multicultural than assimilationist. Nor does pointing the finger at French social policy explain the roots of homegrown jihadism in the United Kingdom. It was in London that Europe's first suicide bombers killed 52 people on the 2005 attacks on the city's transport system. Three of the four bombers were born in in the United Kingdom; the other had been raised there since childhood.

The debate over assimilation versus multiculturalism is not new. For much of the past two decades, French politicians and policymakers had condemned Britain for its multicultural approach, warning that such policies were divisive and failed to create a common set of values or sense of nationhood. As a result, they argued, many Muslims were drawn to Islamism and violence. Now, many of the same arguments have been applied to French social policies.

Most of those drawn toward jihadism are as estranged from Muslim communities as they are from Western societies.

PROBLEM POLICIES

Both sides are, to a degree, correct; French social policies are problematic, and have helped create a more divisive society. But, so have multicultural policies. For too long, politicians and policy makers have debated the differences between the two approaches but ignored the similarities.

British policymakers envisaged their nation as "a community of communities," in the words of the influential Parekh report on multiculturalism, published in 2000. But in doing so, they tended to treat minority communities as if each were a distinct, singular, homogenous, and authentic whole, composed of people speaking with a single voice and view of culture and faith. In other words, policymakers accepted that the United Kingdom was a diverse society, but they sought to manage that diversity by putting people into ethnic and cultural boxes, which where then used to define the needs and rights of those in them. They frequently accepted the most conservative, often religious, figures as the authentic voices of minority groups. Instead of engaging directly with Muslim communities, British authorities effectively delegated responsibility to so-called community leaders.

The consequence has been yet more fragmentation and a more parochial vision of Islam. It is not surprising, then, that most of those drawn toward jihadism are as estranged from Muslim communities as they are from Western societies. Most detest the mores and traditions of their parents and have little time for mainstream, government-sanctioned forms of Islam. Some are led to Islamism, which appears to provide a sense identity that they find neither in mainstream society nor in mainstream Islam. At the fringes, disaffection has become channeled into jihadism. Shaped by black-and-white ideas and values, a few have been drawn to commit acts of horror and to view such acts as part of an existential struggle between Islam and the West.

A cow runs stands in a meadow next to a display advertising the initiative against the construction of new minarets in Switzerland, November 13, 2009.

The irony is that French social policies, which start from a very different point, have ended up creating many of the same problems. France is home to some five million or so French citizens of North African origin. Just 40 percent think of themselves as observant Muslims, and only one in four attend Friday prayers. Yet French politicians, intellectuals, and journalists look at them all as Muslims. Indeed, government ministers, academics, and journalists often cite France's "five million Muslims." The fashion for calling North Africans "Muslim" is relatively recent. In the 1960s and 1970s they may have been labeled beur or arabe (meaning someone from North Africa and Arab, respectively), but rarely Muslim. North African migrants certainly did not define themselves as Muslim; they were mainly secular, often hostile to religion.

The shift toward linking North Africans to Islam is a result of both the greater fracturing of French politics in recent years and the growing perception of Islam as an existential threat to the French republican tradition. French politicians, like those throughout Europe, have faced a public increasingly distrustful of and disengaged from mainstream institutions. And, like those in many European nations, they have attempted to assuage such hostility and resentment by reasserting the notion of a common French identity. Often finding it difficult to articulate clearly the ideas and values that characterize the nation, however, they have instead slipped into defining who the French are not rather than who they are. In this case, Islam is the "other" against which French identity is defined.

"What, in today's France," asks the filmmaker and novelist Karim Miské, "unites the pious Algerian retired worker, the atheist French-Mauritanian director that I am, the Fulani Sufi bank employee from Mantes-la-Jolie, the social worker from Burgundy who has converted to Islam, and the agnostic male nurse who has never set foot in his grandparents' home in Oujda? What brings us together if not the fact that we live within a society which thinks of us as Muslims?"

In principle, the French authorities rejected the United Kingdom's multiculturalist approach. In practice, however, they treated North African migrants and their descendants in a very "multicultural" way—as a single community living alongside another.

The irony is that France's North African population is predominantly secular, and even practicing Muslims are relatively liberal in their views. According to 2011 study by the Institut Français d'Opinion Publique (IFOP), 68 percent of observant women never wear the hijab. Less than a third of practicing Muslims would forbid their daughters from marrying a non-Muslim. Eighty-one percent accept that women should have equal rights in divorce, 44 percent have no problem with cohabitation, 38 percent support the right to abortion, and 31 percent approve of sex before marriage. Homosexuality is the only issue on which there is a majority conservative stance: 77 percent of practicing Muslims disapprove.

Many in the second generation of North African communities are, just like their counterparts in Britain or Belgium, as estranged from their parents' cultures and mores, and from mainstream Islam, as they are from wider French society. And some, as elsewhere in Europe, find their way, to a darker, starker, more tribal vision of Islam. Consider, for instance, Cherif Kouachi, who masterminded the Charlie Hebdo slaughter in Paris in January. He was raised in Gennevilliers, a northern suburb of Paris, home to around 10,000 people of North African origin. He only rarely attended mosque, and appeared not to be particularly religious, but was driven by a sense of social estrangement. He was, according to Mohammed Benali, president of the local mosque, of a "generation that felt excluded, discriminated against, and most of all, humiliated. They spoke and felt French, but were regarded as Arabic; they were culturally confused."

FRACTURED SOCIETIES

Kouachi's story is not that different from that of Mohammad Sidique Khan, the leader of the 7/7 bombings in London. Nor is that different from the story of Abdelhamid Abaaoud, the mastermind of the Paris attacks. Abaaoud grew up in Molenbeek, the Brussels ghetto that has become a byword for poverty, unemployment, and radical Islamism. Abaaoud attended, however, one of Belgium's top secondary schools, Saint-Pierre d'Uccle. He dropped out of school and stopped visiting the local mosque, as did his close friend Salah Abdeslam, another of the Paris gunmen. The imams were too steeped in tradition for their tastes. "So they look elsewhere," says Olivier Vanderhaegen, who works in a local project to combat youth radicalization.

Social policies in Belgium, France, and the United Kingdom aimed at fostering integration are all different. What they have in common, though, is that all have helped create a more fractured society, and all have helped entrench narrower visions of belongingness and identity. Neither assimilationist nor multicultural policies have created Islamism or jihadism. What they have done is helped create the space for Islamism to flourish, and to funnel disaffection into jihadism.

KENAN MALIK is a writer, lecturer, and broadcaster. His latest book is *The Quest for a Moral Compass: A Global History of Ethics*.

© Foreign Affairs

ISIS' Next Target

Terrorism After Brussels

Robin Simcox

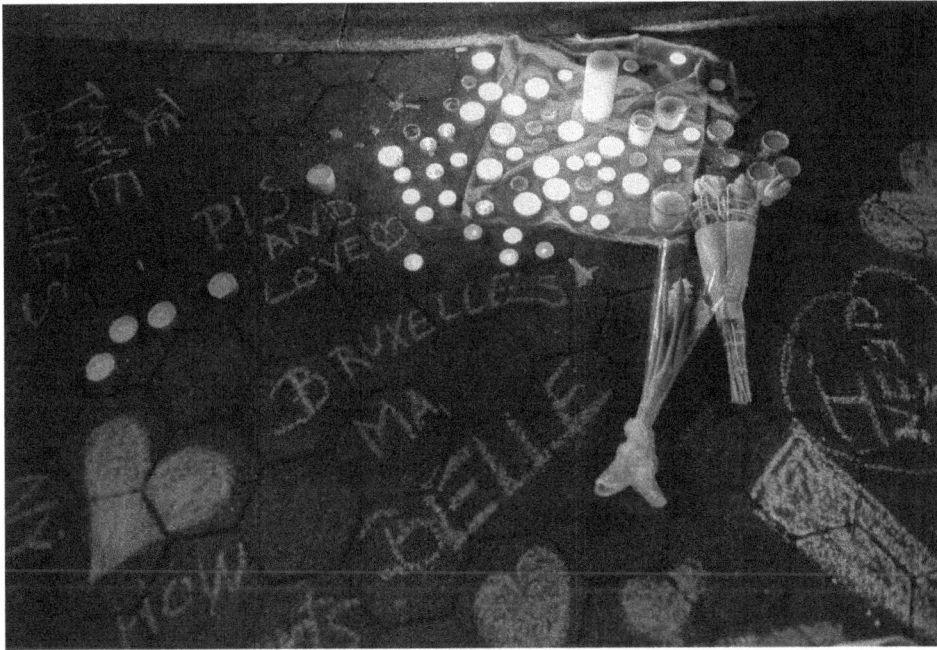

People gather at a makeshift memorial for the victims of the Belgium attacks in Brussels, in Union Square in the Manhattan borough in New York, March 22, 2016.

The recent attacks in Brussels show that terrorists' ability to strike at the heart of Europe remains apparently undiminished. Early reports suggest a death toll of around 31, with more than 100 injured. The Islamic State (ISIS) has claimed responsibility for the attack.

Belgium may seem an unlikely hub of jihadism, but despite being a small and peaceful nation, Belgian connections to militancy are long established. In the 1990s, bullets and guns made their way from local jihadi crooks in Brussels to the Groupe Islamique Armé, Algerian terrorists aiming to establish an Islamic state in Algeria.

Throughout that decade, a smattering of Belgian residents headed off to fight in various foreign conflicts, including the one in Chechnya.

After 9/11, a major terrorism trial in Belgium led to the convictions of over 20 Islamists. Those jailed included Nizar Trabelsi, a former professional soccer player who had joined al Qaeda and planned to commit a suicide attack against a NATO air base. It also included Tarek Maaroufi, who was linked to the assassination of Ahmed Shah Massoud, the Afghan military leader whose death served as al Qaeda's warm-up act two days before its main event.

More recently, as the war in Syria metastasized, Belgians were drawn there in significant numbers. Of the 5,000-6,000 Europeans who fought in Syria, up to 553 are believed to be Belgian. That makes the country the home of the highest number of foreign fighters in Syria, per capita, of any Western European country. Small wonder that even the country's justice minister admits that his country has "a foreign fighters problem." Some of those who arranged for the travel of these fighters to Syria were convicted of terrorism in a Belgian court in February 2015.

By most estimates, over 100 Belgians have now returned from the conflict. Although that is concerning enough, it must also be placed in the context of a broader issue. The Schengen Agreement allows for virtually unhindered freedom of movement throughout much of Europe, something that jihadists have taken advantage of time and again. A fighter from the Syrian jihad who is returning to Germany or France poses as much of a danger to Belgium as one who was born and bred in Brussels. The threat is continent-wide, and approximately 2,000 fighters are thought have returned to Europe.

Despite all this, there may still be some bewilderment about the choice of Belgium as a target of ISIS' latest attack in Europe. It is not a leading military power like France or the United Kingdom. Yet Belgium is absolutely central to ISIS' aims to carry out attacks in Europe in the hope of inspiring new recruits to their cause. After all, it was Brussels that first suffered casualties from the foreign fighters returning from Syria: Mehdi Nemmouche, who fought for ISIS in Syria, shot and killed four at the Jewish Museum in Brussels in May 2014.

Belgium was also the site of the first attack in Europe directed by ISIS, as opposed to just being inspired by the group. It was in Verviers, eastern Belgium, last January that ISIS first displayed its talent for getting trained fighters back into Europe from Syria, loading them up with weapons and bombs, and directing them to attempt a major attack. The cell had acquired AK-47s, explosives, walkie-talkies, and GoPro cameras. A Belgian federal prosecutor commented that the cell was plotting "imminent terrorist attacks on a grand scale." Fortunately, those plans were thwarted. The Belgians had been tracking the cell for weeks and after a dramatic shootout, killed two terrorists and captured another.

Factors relevant to both the Jewish Museum and Verviers plotters would reappear in the months following. The first was the presence of a Belgian national called Abdelhamid Abaaoud, whom investigators regarded as the link between ISIS' leadership in Syria and their operations in Europe. Abaaoud was in contact with both Nemmouche and the Verviers cell.

The second was that the men all had ties to Molenbeek, the deprived district of Brussels that has been a constant feature in terrorism investigations. This district—an impoverished area rife with unemployment and heavily populated by immigrants—has come up time and again in ISIS-linked terror activities. Ayoub el-Khazzani, who tried to gun down passengers on a train destined for Paris last August, stayed in Molenbeek. Police launched a major raid there after the Paris attacks last November, since many of the perpetrators lived there. Salah Abdeslam, one of the plotters involved in that attack, was arrested after a raid in Molenbeek just days ago.

Abaaoud was killed last November in a raid in Paris. Yet the problems in Molenbeek go way beyond those posed by ISIS and speak to a broader European problem of multiculturalism and effectively integrating newcomers. At a time when Europe is taking in more than a million refugees and economic migrants a year, solving the problem cannot be treated urgently enough. It is a problem that may take generations to resolve.

In the short-term, then, the priority is to get a fix on the size of ISIS' European network. The group has been allowed to lay down roots in multiple cities. ISIS, or groups and individuals inspired by it, has now struck in France on multiple occasions, and in Belgium and Denmark. Plots have been thwarted in Austria, Italy, Spain, and the United Kingdom. Intelligence agencies have had many successes after 9/11, but the number of attacks getting through is quickly increasing; another successful ISIS attack is almost inevitable. Yet all that European leaders can offer so far are regurgitations of the need for greater EU intelligence sharing.

ISIS has made a bet that Europe's problems—concerns over the integration of Muslim populations throughout the continent, a lack of clear national identity, open borders, and an overwhelmed security apparatus—run very, very deep. It is wagering that the situation there will become so desperate that it can wage a war for the souls of European Muslims, presenting them with a binary choice of apostasy or support for their Caliphate. It is a bet they will surely lose. Yet the bloodshed that will take place on the way should make us fear what lies ahead for Europe in the years to come.

ROBIN SIMCOX is Margaret Thatcher Fellow at the Heritage Foundation.

© Foreign Affairs

The French Connection

Explaining Sunni Militancy Around the World

William McCants and Christopher Meserole

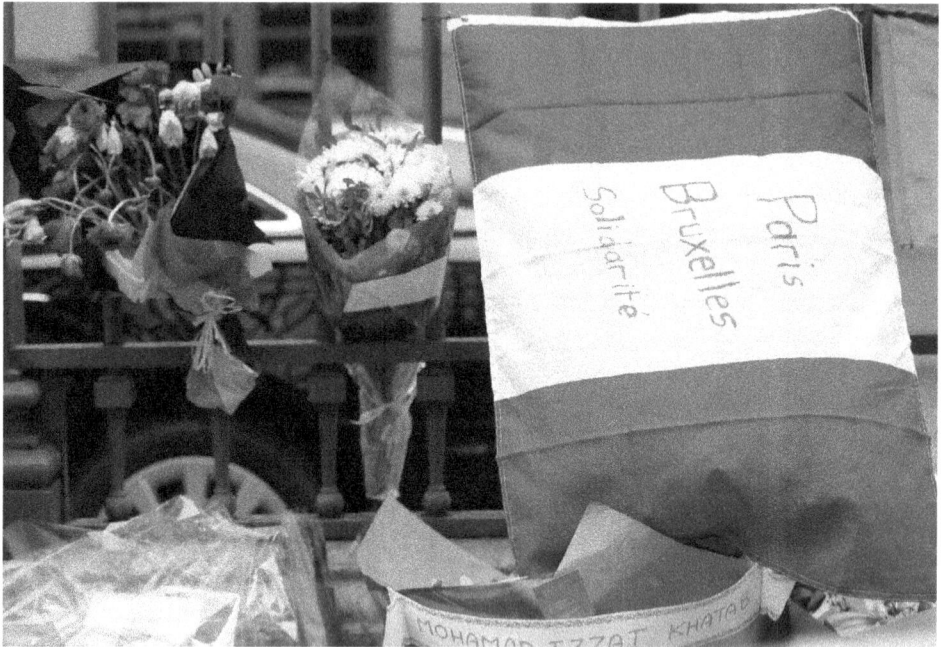

A French flag with the message 'Paris Brussels Solidarity' is displayed next to flowers with the colors of the Belgium flag in front of the Belgium embassy in Paris, France, March 23, 2016.

The mass causality terrorist attacks in Paris and now in Brussels underscore an unsettling truth: Jihadists pose a greater threat to France and Belgium than to the rest of Europe. The body counts are larger and the disrupted plots are more numerous. The trend might be explained by the nature of the Islamic State (ISIS) networks in Europe or as failures of policing in France and Belgium. Both explanations have merit. However, our research reveals that another factor may be at play: French political culture.

Last fall, we began a project to test empirically the many proposed explanations for Sunni militancy around the globe. The goal was to take common measures of the violence—namely, the number of Sunni foreign fighters from any given country as well as the number of Sunni terror attacks carried out within it—and then crunch the numbers to see which explanations best predicted a country's rate of Sunni radicalization and violence. (The raw foreign fighter data came from The International Centre for the Study of Radicalisation and Political Violence; the original attack data came from the University of Maryland's START project.)

What we found surprised us, particularly when it came to foreign fighter radicalization. It turns out that the best predictor of foreign fighter radicalization was not a country's wealth. Nor was it how well-educated its citizens were, how healthy they were, or even how much Internet access they enjoyed. Instead, the top predictor was whether a country was Francophone; that is, whether it currently lists (or previously listed) French as a national language. As strange as it may seem, four of the five countries with the highest rates of radicalization in the world are Francophone, including the top two in Europe (France and Belgium).

REUTERS

An Islamic State fighter gestures from a vehicle in the countryside of the Syrian Kurdish town of Kobani, after the Islamic State fighters took control of the area, October 7, 2014.

Knowledgeable readers will immediately object that the raw numbers tell a different story. The English-speaking United Kingdom, for example, has produced far more foreign fighters than French-speaking Belgium. And fighters from Saudi Arabia number in the several thousands. But the raw numbers are misleading. If you view the foreign fighters as a percentage of the overall Muslim population, you see a different picture. Per Muslim resident, Belgium produces far more foreign fighters than either the United Kingdom or Saudi Arabia.

So what could the language of love possibly have to do with Islamist violence? We suspect that it is really a proxy for something else: French political culture. The French approach to secularism is more aggressive than, say, the British approach. France and Belgium, for example, are the only two countries in Europe to ban the full veil in their public schools. They're also the only two countries in Western Europe not to gain the highest rating for democracy in the well-known Polity score data, which does not include explanations for the markdowns.

Adding support to this story are the top interactions we found between different variables. When you look at which combination of variables is most predictive, it turns out that the "Francophone effect" is actually strongest in the countries that are most developed: French-speaking countries with the highest literacy, best infrastructure, and best health system. This is not a story about French colonial plunder. If anything, it's a story about what happens when French economic and political development has most deeply taken root.

An important subplot within this story concerns the distribution of wealth. In particular, the rate of youth unemployment and urbanization appear to matter a great deal too. Globally, we found that when between 10 and 30 percent of a country's youth are unemployed, there is a strong relationship between a rise in youth unemployment and a rise in Sunni militancy. Rates outside that range don't have an effect. Likewise, when urbanization is between 60 and 80 percent, there is a strong relationship.

These findings seem to matter most in Francophone countries. Among the over 1,000 interactions our model looked at, those between Francophone and youth unemployment and Francophone and urbanization both ranked among the 15 most predictive. There's broad anecdotal support for this idea: consider the rampant radicalization in Molenbeek, in the Paris banlieus, in Ben Gardane. Each of these contexts have produced a massively disproportionate share of foreign fighters, and each are also urban pockets with high youth unemployment.

Broken windows of the terminal at Brussels airport are seen during a ceremony following bomb attacks in Brussels in Zaventem, Belgium, March 23, 2016.

As with the Francophone finding overall, we're left with guesswork as to why exactly the relationships between French politics, urbanization, youth unemployment, and Sunni militancy exist. We suspect that when there are large numbers of unemployed youth, some of them are bound to get up to mischief. When they live in large cities, they have more opportunities to connect with people espousing radical causes. And when those cities are in Francophone countries that adopt the strident French approach to secularism, Sunni radicalism is more appealing.

For now, the relationship needs to be studied and tested by comparing several cases in countries and between countries. We also found other interesting relationships—such as between Sunni violence and prior civil conflict—but they are neither as strong nor as compelling.

Regardless, the latest attacks in Belgium are reason enough to share the initial findings. They may be way off, but at least they are based on the best available data. If the data is wrong or our interpretations skewed, we hope the effort will lead to more rigorous explanations of what is driving jihadist terrorism in Europe. Our initial findings should in no way imply that Francophone countries are responsible for the recent horrible attacks—no country deserves to have its civilians killed, regardless of the perpetrator's motives. But the magnitude of the violence and the fear it engenders demand that we investigate those motives beyond just the standard boilerplate explanations.

CHRISTOPHER MESEROLE is a Pre-Doctoral Fellow at Brookings Foreign Policy. WILLIAM McCANTS is author of *The ISIS Apocalypse* and Director of the Project on U.S. Relations with the Islamic World at the Brookings Institution.

The French Disconnection

Francophone Countries and Radicalization

Olivier Decottignies

Members of the Muslim community in Belgium take part in a ceremony to commemorate the victims of last month's attacks on the city's Zaventem airport and the Maelbeek metro station, outside the station in Brussels, Belgium, April 9, 2016.

In a recent article, William McCants and Christopher Meserole, both from the Brookings Institution, argue that "the best predictor" of foreign fighter radicalization is whether their country of origin is Francophone. Rather than incriminating the French language as such, the authors see a connection between radicalization and what they call "French political culture." They lay special emphasis on the "strident" and "aggressive" French approach to secularism. Radicalization in Belgium and France, in their view, fit into a pattern that they say holds true with other Francophone countries, in particular the most economically developed.

McCants and Meserole's indictment of "French political culture" negates the diversity of the Francophone world; think of an "English political culture" that would encompass, say, the United States, the Palau Islands, and Robert Mugabe's Zimbabwe. Sentences such as "If anything, it's a story of what happens when French economic and political development has most deeply taken root" also carry unsavory undertones. For comparison, replace "French" with "Arab," "Latino," or any other group.

If anything, the McCants-Meserole thesis illustrates the pitfalls of data-based analysis in the study of terrorism. Although the two scholars initially aimed at "explaining the Sunni militancy around the world," they ended up focusing on a couple of European countries that together make up slightly more than one percent of the world's population. The authors then narrow their focus from Francophone countries in general to wealthy Francophone countries in particular and, finally, to wealthy Francophone countries with an "aggressive" approach to secularism. Out of 29 states that have French as an official language, the piece fails to name any others besides Belgium and France.

YVES HERMAN / REUTERS

Federal prosecutor spokesperson Eric Van Der Sypt addresses a news conference on a suspect in the attack which took place at the Brussels international airport of Zaventem, as CCTV images of the man can be seen on a screen in Brussels, Belgium April 7, 2016.

McCants' remarkable work on the Islamic State (ISIS) in its Middle Eastern heartland drew on his knowledge of the region and, indeed, its languages. However, this recent study displays a surprisingly shallow understanding of the French-speaking world. To start with, Francophones are actually a minority in Belgium, where Flemish speakers make up nearly 60 percent of the country's overall population. And Flanders accounts for more Belgian jihadi foreign fighters than French-speaking Wallonia. Besides, regardless of their whereabouts and linguistic affiliation, Belgian citizens of Turkish descent seem less likely than Belgians of Moroccan origin to embrace violent radicalism. French political culture cannot explain both things.

The assumption that Belgium and France share the same "French political culture" does not hold either. France is a unitary although increasingly decentralized republic, whereas Belgium is a federal kingdom with a high degree of devolution on linguistic and regional lines. The two countries also diverge markedly in their approach to religion. The French Constitution declares that "The Republic neither recognizes, nor salaries, nor subsidizes any religion." On the other hand, the Belgian state officially recognizes several religions, including Islam, pays the wages of ministers, and offers religious education in public schools. Besides, Sweden, considered by many a model of multiculturalism in Europe, has fewer foreign fighters per capita than Belgium, but more than secular France.

Even McCants and Meserole's assertion that France and Belgium enforce a "ban of the full veil in their public schools" is inaccurate. Both countries do ban the full-face veil in public spaces. But whereas conspicuous religious symbols of all faiths (including Jewish yarmulkes, Sikh turbans, or large crosses) are banned in all French public schools, in Belgium, rules are defined at the local level. And in both Belgium and France, the decision to ban full-face veils in 2011 came as a response to the expansion of the Salafist interpretation of Islam, which was hardly a French export.

OLIVIER DECOTTIGNIES, a French career diplomat, is a Diplomat in Residence at The Washington Institute for Near East Policy. The opinions expressed are his alone.

The Myth of Lone-Wolf Terrorism

The Attacks in Europe and Digital Extremism

Daveed Gartenstein-Ross and Nathaniel Barr

A man types on a keyboard in front of a computer screen on which an Islamic State flag is displayed, in this picture illustration taken in Zenica, Bosnia and Herzegovina, February 6, 2016.

This month, Europe has again been rocked by a series of shocking terrorist attacks perpetrated by lone individuals and claimed in the name of the Islamic State (ISIS). On July 14, Mohamed Lahouaiej Bouhlel, a Tunisian national residing in France, killed over 80 and wounded hundreds when he ploughed a 19-ton cargo truck through crowds celebrating Bastille Day in the southern French city of Nice. Mere days after the Nice massacre, a 17-year-old Afghan migrant seeking asylum in Germany attacked passengers on a train in Würzburg with an axe and a knife, wounding four before police killed him. Two other attacks claimed in ISIS' name have been carried out since then: A suicide bombing on July 24 injured 15 in the German city of Ansbach, and on July 26, two attackers claiming allegiance to ISIS stormed a church in a suburb of the French city of Rouen, slit an 84-year-old priest's throat, and took hostages.

These incidents are part of a broader trend of increasing violence carried out by lone individuals. Analysts, journalists, and scholars have been quick to label each perpetrator of recent attacks as a lone wolf: individuals who lacked substantial connections to ISIS or other jihadist groups and who carried out their operations without the assistance of others. The designation has generally been applied within 24 hours of these attacks, before significant intelligence about an incident's planning and execution has emerged—and long before authorities have concluded their investigation. Indeed, less than a day after the Nice attack, observers rushed to describe Lahouaiej Bouhlel as a lone wolf who was not in fact linked to ISIS.

Observers have repeatedly erred by definitively categorizing attacks as lone-wolf operations when they would later turn out to be connected to broader cells or networks. At a minimum, individuals labeled lone wolves are often in communication with other militants, sometimes using encrypted services that are difficult to detect and decipher. There is a danger in rushing to label operatives as disconnected from others, as doing so can cause analysts to overlook the networks that facilitate and encourage attacks. It is time to put the myth of the lone wolf to rest.

CHARLES PLATIAU / REUTERS

French police and anti-crime brigade (BAC) secure a street they carried out a counter-terrorism swoop at different locations in Argenteuil, a suburb north of Paris, France, July 21, 2016.

MISSING NETWORKS

The tendency to view lone attackers as unconnected to the broader ISIS organization prevented observers from fully comprehending the magnitude of the network that was behind the complex coordinated attacks in Paris and Brussels.

In April 2015, Sid Ahmed Ghlam, an Algerian national studying in France, called for medical help after accidentally shooting himself in the leg while handling a firearm. Authorities' investigation revealed that Ghlam, who was in possession of several guns, was planning to attack churches in the Paris area and may have been involved in the murder of a woman found dead in a Paris suburb. In August 2015, three Americans restrained Ayoub El-Khazzani, a 25-year old Moroccan national, before he could open fire on passengers traveling by train from Amsterdam to Paris.

At the time, the two attacks were seen as disconnected, with Khazzani generally labeled a lone wolf. And the bumbling incompetence of both incidents—Ghlam shot himself, while Khazzani's weapon jammed before he could get off a shot—made the attacks seem like the work of rank amateurs. Meanwhile, ISIS fueled perceptions that it was primarily interested in inspiring lone-wolf attacks rather than guiding them, with a pro-ISIS media outlet producing a propaganda video shortly after Khazzani's botched attack calling on "lone lions" to kill the group's enemies.

But after the devastating November 2015 attacks in Paris, it became clear that initial judgments had been wrong. A March 2016 The New York Times article by Rukmini Callimachi detailed how Abdelhamid Abaaoud, the ground commander of the Paris attacks, had directed Ghlam, Khazzani, and several others to carry out attacks in Europe, even as he was preparing the Paris operation. Although he of course wanted these small-scale plots to succeed, they also helped deflect attention from ISIS' more sophisticated operational planning, serving as a "smoke screen" that allowed the group to "calmly prepare" its future operations, in the words of one French official. Because counterterrorism analysts and officials viewed Ghlam, Khazzani, and other attackers as unrelated to one another, they did not identify the operational infrastructure involved in coordinating ISIS' various attacks in Europe.

With the social media boom and the growth in encrypted communications, radicalization and operational planning can easily take place entirely online.

The failure to identify common ties between supposed lone wolves and ISIS is part of a broader and long-standing pattern of underestimating the scope of jihadist networks in the West. An official inquiry into the July 7, 2005, terrorist attacks in

London, for example, described the cell that carried it out as autonomous and self-actuating rather than tied to al Qaeda. One British official stated that "the London attacks were a modest, simple affair by four seemingly normal men using the internet." But the idea that the London bombings were completely unrelated to al Qaeda was definitively refuted by a commemorative video the jihadist group later released in July 2006, which showed footage of a martyrdom tape recorded by cell leader Mohammad Sidique Khan. On the tape, al Qaeda's then-deputy emir, Ayman al-Zawahiri, also claimed that Khan and fellow plotter Shehzad Tanweer had visited one of al Qaeda's training camps in Pakistan "seeking martyrdom," an account that has since been corroborated by Western intelligence agencies. Bob Ayers, a security expert at London's Chatham House think tank, commented when the new video was released, "It makes the police look pretty bad. It means the investigation was either wrong, or they identified links but were reluctant to reveal them." Since then, officials and analysts have often continued to ignore attackers' ties with broader networks. Part of the reason for the consistent failure may lie in a desire to avoid culpability; observers may perceive attacks carried out by networks as something officials should have prevented, but potential lone attackers are notoriously difficult to spot. Another reason may be a desire to downplay networks due to policy preferences, such as wanting to avoid taking kinetic action against the networks driving these attacks. But it is a mistake to conflate facts with policy preferences, and the truth is that terrorists' ties to broader networks are frequently overlooked.

In fact, theories that recent attacks were the work of individuals are already being discredited. When ISIS claimed responsibility for the July 2016 Würzburg train attack, the group released a video featuring the perpetrator that demonstrated ISIS had advance knowledge that he intended to strike. Less than a week after the Nice attack, French authorities revealed that Lahouaiej Bouhlel may not have acted alone. Several individuals, whom prosecutors also described as having jihadist sympathies, were detained in connection with the massacre. One suspect had posed for pictures in the truck that Lahouaiej Bouhlel drove through a celebrating crowd. Further, the perpetrator, who had been planning the attack for months, had sent out a text message to an alleged coconspirator just minutes before the attack requesting "more weapons."

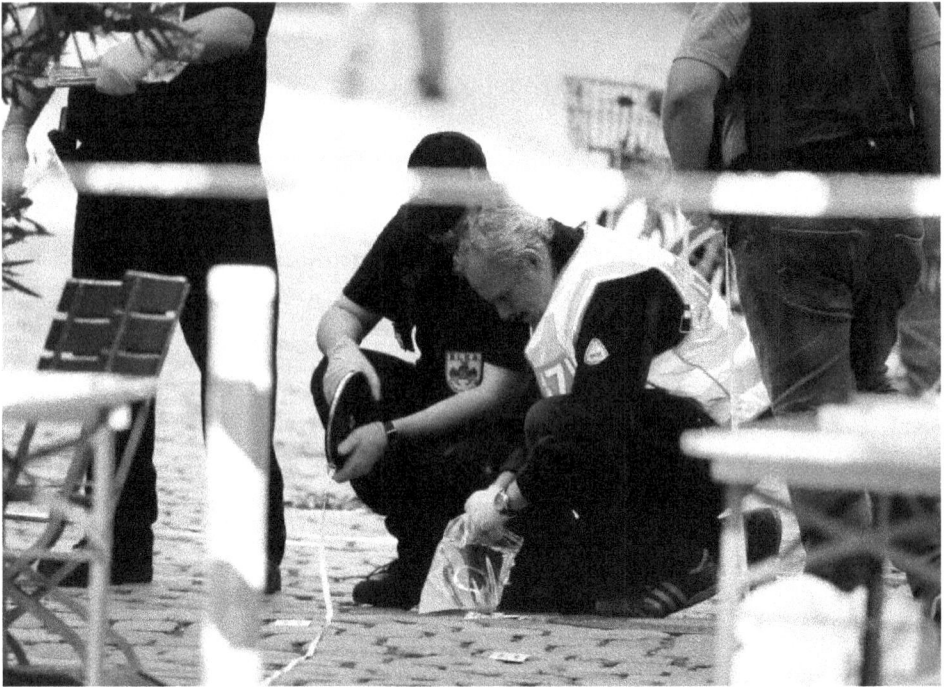

Police secure the area after an explosion in Ansbach, Germany, July 25, 2016.

DIGITAL DILEMMA

The nature of radicalization and operational planning in the digital age has complicated efforts to interpret and analyze attacks perpetrated by single individuals. Jihadists plotting murders in the West used to congregate in person, meeting in small groups in underground mosques, houses, or other discrete locations. Radicalization occurred through in-person contact. Counterterrorism officials looked for physical hubs of recruitment, tapping phones and scanning surveillance videos for evidence that cells were meeting.

But with the social media boom and the growth in encrypted communications, radicalization and operational planning can easily take place entirely online. ISIS has capitalized on evolving communications technologies, building cohesive online communities that foster a sense of "remote intimacy" and thus facilitate radicalization. The group has also established a team of "virtual planners" who use the Internet to identify recruits, and to coordinate and direct attacks, often without meeting the perpetrators in person. Junaid Hussain, a British ISIS operative who was killed in August 2015, played the role of virtual planner for the May 2015 strike against the Draw Muhammad contest in Garland, Texas. Hussain had communicated online with Elton Simpson before the attack and was the first to celebrate it on social media. It may take months—or longer—to detect the role of virtual planners in attacks.

The changing nature of operational planning underscores the need for a new paradigm for understanding the relationship between single attackers and networks. It no longer makes sense to apply pre-digital-age thinking to jihadist attacks perpetrated in the age of Twitter, Telegram, and end-to-end encryption.

Instead, it is useful to think of four categories of attacks, with descending connections to a network. The first category consists of operations in which the attacker was trained and dispatched by an organization. Reda Hame, who traveled to Syria and received weapons training from Abaaoud before being sent back to Europe, perfectly fits this mold. The second category is attackers in touch via social media with virtual planners such as Hussain, who help set targets, determine the timing of the attack, and provide technical assistance. The third category is operatives who are in contact with a militant group via online communications but do not receive specific instructions about carrying out an attack. Finally, the fourth category comprises the true lone wolves, individuals who strike without ever communicating with jihadist networks, either online or in person.

It is clear that extremely few of the jihadists labeled lone wolves truly fit that definition. As long as attacks are falsely categorized though, the world can't even begin to fight back. We need a better model for understanding terrorism in the digital age.

DAVEED GARTENSTEIN-ROSS is a senior fellow at the Foundation for Defense of Democracies and the chief executive officer of Valens Global. NATHANIEL BARR is the research manager at Valens Global.

Keeping Europe Safe

Counterterrorism for the Continent

David Omand

En garde! Near the Eiffel Tower, Paris, March 2016.

Just before 11 PM on Thursday, July 14, a 19-ton truck turned onto a seaside promenade in Nice, France, where crowds had gathered to watch Bastille Day fireworks. The truck sped up, plowing into the people on the promenade. By the time French police shot the driver, the truck had traveled 1.1 miles, killing 84 people and injuring hundreds more. That attack came less than four months after three terrorists killed 32 people in explosions in the departure hall of Brussels Airport and a metro car near Brussels' Maelbeek subway station. And it came eight months after a group of young men killed 130 people in Paris, in the deadliest attack on France since World War II. The self-proclaimed Islamic State, or ISIS, claimed responsibility for all three attacks.

These attacks have exposed deep flaws in continental Europe's approach to counterterrorism. European intelligence agencies do not share information with one another fast enough. Europe's porous borders allow terrorists to cross the continent with ease. Other European governments have lagged behind the United Kingdom in developing capabilities and legal frameworks for digital intelligence gathering and in cultivating effective cooperation between their many agencies.

In the aftermath of the attacks, continental Europe now has a unique opportunity to reform its intelligence infrastructure. Its leaders recognize the need for action. After the Paris attacks, French President François Hollande imposed a state of emergency, declaring that "France is at war." A French parliamentary commission of inquiry into the Paris attack concluded that Europe was not up to the task of fighting terrorism, identifying failures in French intelligence and in the communication between intelligence and law enforcement bodies. Belgian authorities have accepted that their counterterrorism policies are inadequate: the Belgian interior and justice ministers offered their resignations over the evident failures in Belgian intelligence.

European governments must now commit to lasting reforms, ramping up investment and breaking down barriers to information sharing. The United Kingdom's vote to leave the EU will not make things easier. Yet it also creates an opportunity to create other, stronger networks for international cooperation across the continent and beyond.

As they respond to ISIS' threat, governments would do well to heed four main lessons from history. Governments must not forget the importance of understanding the enemy, formulating realistic goals that are consistent with democratic values, remaining flexible in the face of a threat that is unlikely to remain static, and, above all, forging partnerships based on earned trust.

UNDERSTAND THE ENEMY

Episodes from the 1990s and early years of this century illustrate the first key lesson of successful counterterrorism: the importance of understanding the nature of the threat. When intelligence agencies misdiagnose the danger after a plot is uncovered or after an attack, governments are less likely to invest to preempt future threats.

Throughout the 1990s, despite several warning signs, British and U.S. intelligence agencies failed to grasp the potential significance of the threat from Islamist terrorist groups. In 2000, the British Security Service uncovered the first cell of Islamist bomb-makers in the United Kingdom. But it treated the discovery as a one-off event, since at the time it did not seem similar to other threats that the intelligence agency had encountered. Later that year, the Security Service arrested a Pakistani microbiologist who was seeking pathogen samples and equipment suspected to be suitable for making biological weapons. Once again, however, the intelligence agency viewed the episode as an isolated incident. In fact, British and U.S. intelligence agencies later discovered that it was part of an al Qaeda plan to develop biological weapons. It would not be until after 9/11 that the British intelligence and security community would grasp the potential scale of the threat from radicalized extremists and would invest enough resources in response.

Many European intelligence agencies have been slow to recognize the threat that ISIS poses.

The U.S. intelligence community was similarly slow to understand the extent of the danger al Qaeda posed. In January 1993, Mir Aimal Kansi, a Pakistani jihadist, shot two CIA employees outside the agency's headquarters, in Langley, Virginia. The CIA responded by fortifying its perimeter security, but its assessment of its counterterrorism strategy did not change. Just one month later, an al Qaeda truck bomb exploded under the North Tower of the World Trade Center, killing six but failing to topple the building. Intelligence agencies tend not to examine the causes of a near miss as seriously as they do the causes of an actual disaster. (Airlines, by contrast, routinely scour close calls for lessons.) Thus, after the 1993 attacks, they learned valuable tactical lessons—how to protect a building from attack, for example—but missed the larger message: that al Qaeda was actively plotting to cause mass casualties on U.S. soil.

Five years later, al Qaeda blew up the U.S. embassies in Kenya and Tanzania, killing more than 200 people. Within weeks, U.S. President Bill Clinton ordered cruise missile strikes on targets in Afghanistan and Sudan. Osama bin Laden became a high-priority intelligence target. But the U.S. government still massively underestimated the risk of a terrorist attack on the United States itself and did little to strengthen homeland security; the subsequent attacks on 9/11 came as all the more of a shock.

When intelligence agencies understand the threat they face, they're more likely to adopt prudent reforms. In April 1993, the Provisional Irish Republican Army detonated a massive truck bomb in the City of London, inflicting more than $700 million worth of damage, killing one, and injuring 44. The British authorities, who understood the nature of the threat after decades spent fighting the IRA, assessed that the group had the explosives, personnel, and funds to continue to pose a danger. The case for boosting investment in security was clear. Within a few months, the British government had set up the "ring of steel," a security cordon of checkpoints and surveillance cameras around the City of London that covered every entry point and major building. The police, local government, and private companies worked together to make London's infrastructure more resilient.

France also successfully adapted its counterterrorism strategy after the Armed Islamic Group launched a series of attacks in the 1990s, hoping to deter France from intervening in the group's struggle to seize power in Algeria. The French authorities understood the group's motives and the methods it was likely to use and rapidly strengthened France's security apparatus. The government made it a crime to associate with terrorists, by providing them with a vehicle, for instance, and introduced flexible pretrial procedures led by specialized counterterrorism magistrates and trials in dedicated courts. These moves made it easier to convict terrorists and deprived them of local support.

A Belgian soldier patrols a shopping street in central Brussels following the Paris attacks, Belgium, November 2015.

Today, however, many European intelligence agencies have been slow to recognize the threat that ISIS poses. They have largely failed to combine the work of their domestic and external intelligence services and have failed to integrate the work of the police with that of their security and intelligence agencies. For too long, they have ignored the risks inherent in the Schengen system of open borders, which leaves their security dependent on the effective intelligence of their neighbors. As a result, networks of terrorists, hardened by fighting in Iraq and Syria, in possession of European passports, and hiding among Europe's many undocumented refugees, now reach across the continent.

KEEP CALM

The second lesson is the importance of setting a clear and realistic strategic aim, one that European governments can meet while staying true to their democratic values. After 9/11, U.S. President George W. Bush declared that his administration would do whatever it took to destroy al Qaeda. He authorized measures unheard of in peacetime, including extraordinary rendition, detention without trial, torture, and the targeted killing of enemy combatants far from any recog-nized battlefield.

Yet much of the United States' response to 9/11 has proved counterproductive. The rhetoric of the so-called war on terror expressed resolve, but it led policymakers to overreact in their desperation to secure "wins." Prevailing in a long war is not the same as winning tactical engagements or even a battle or two, and many of the extraordinary measures the United States implemented, such as the use of torture, helped reinforce extremist narratives and damaged the United States' standing in the world. The invasion and occupation of Iraq helped produce a new generation of terrorists. The Bush-era drone program, which President Barack Obama has since expanded, has killed much of al Qaeda's senior leadership and disrupted its ability to mount organized attacks. But the organization still represents a significant threat through its links to the al-Nusra Front in Syria, and the inevitable accidental killings of civilians in drone strikes have provided ready material for extremist propaganda.

The 9/11 attacks also shocked the British government. (Sixty-seven British citizens died that day, the largest single loss of British life in a terrorist attack.) At first, the United Kingdom responded in a similar fashion to the United States; by October, U.S. and British armed forces were fighting alongside each other in Afghanistan. But their counterterrorism strategies soon diverged. As the United States pressed on with its "war on terror," the British government adopted a counterterrorism strategy known as CONTEST, which aimed to "reduce the risk to the UK and its interests overseas from terrorism, so that people can go about their lives freely and with confidence." The government sought to reassure tourists, encourage investment, and stabilize markets. This approach emphasized the continuation and resumption of ordinary life. In contrast, the United States, in adopting extreme measures, preserved an abnormal situation, playing into the terrorists' narrative.

DYLAN MARTINEZ / REUTERS

The number 30 double-decker bus after the 7/7 attacks in Tavistock Square in central London, July 8, 2005.

So far, the British approach has worked. Since 9/11, there has been only one major successful attack in the United Kingdom: the bombings on London's public transport on July 7, 2005, which killed 52 people. But the threat remains severe. British intelligence has thwarted several major al Qaeda attacks, including a sophisticated attempt to down U.S. airliners over the Atlantic in 2006. In February, the British security minister said that at least seven attacks had been stopped in the previous 18 months alone. Through tight cooperation between the Security Service and the police, supported by the other British intelligence agencies, the government has successfully identified and prosecuted hundreds of terrorists (there were 255 terrorism-related arrests in just one year, between March 2015 and March 2016) without significantly infringing civil liberties.

This lesson is an important one for Europe's current leaders. Since the attacks in Paris and Brussels, governments have ramped up protection at crowded public events. But there are limits to what they can do. A combination of effective intelligence and protective security measures can almost eliminate the risk of attack for a small number of high-value targets, such as a world leader or a nuclear power station. (ISIS may well be considering such targets; last November, investigators found video footage at the apartment of a militant linked to the Paris terrorist attack of a senior official at a Belgian nuclear facility.)

Yet there will always be a risk that terrorists will instead focus on softer targets— subway stations, cultural centers, concert venues—as they have recently done in Denmark, Belgium, and France. In response, authorities should do what they can to ensure that people feel safe when they use public transportation or congregate in public spaces, even if the government cannot eliminate the risk. They should deploy more armed police officers to areas of high risk and train rapid-response units to react to the sorts of attacks that have hit Mumbai, Nairobi, Copenhagen, Paris, and Brussels, where small groups of armed men have rampaged across the city.

Continental Europe now has a unique opportunity to reform its intelligence infrastructure.

States of emergency, such as the one France imposed, can empower authorities to take sensible immediate steps to protect the public. But they do not represent a long-term answer. If measures such as the widespread deployment of soldiers on the streets persist for too long, authorities risk creating a new normal—one that the public will think terrorists have imposed on them.

When officials communicate with the public about the risk of terrorism, they should temper expectations. It is difficult to stop those who are prepared to use extreme violence in the pursuit of an ideological end, especially if they are willing to die for their cause. Statements that pledge to eliminate the risk of a future attack may promise too much—and they may convince publics to accept weaker protections of their human rights in the pursuit of absolute security. Instead, governments should provide a truthful and convincing narrative to explain the causes of the attacks and lay out a clear road map for what the public can expect next.

ADAPT AND EVOLVE

A third lesson is that policymakers must remain open to adapting their strategies and methods as the jihadist threat evolves. To become more flexible, intelligence agencies should adopt a joint approach to counterterrorism, just as modern armed forces rely on joint mission planning and command. In 2003, for example, the United Kingdom created the Joint Terrorism Analysis Centre, in which staff from the intelligence agencies, the police, the military, and other government agencies analyze and process information together. One year later, the U.S. government launched a similar organization, the National Counterterrorism Center. The French parliamentary commission of inquiry set up after the 2015 Paris attack has called for the French government to establish a similar joint organization in Paris to overcome coordination problems between the many French police services and security agencies.

STEPHANE DE SAKUTIN / REUTERS

French President Francois Hollande delivers a speech on constitutional reform and the fight against terrorism at the Elysee Palace in Paris, France, March 2016.

The British Security Service provides a case study in how an intelligence agency can become more flexible. After the July 2005 attack in London, the agency set up eight regional counterterrorism hubs, based alongside police counterterrorism units, outside the city in the places it considered most vulnerable to radicalization. By decentralizing its investigations and cooperating closely with regional police departments, the Security Service could better understand local communities. Other countries affected by jihadist radicalization should consider this model. In a promising first step, France has already announced the creation of a dozen regional "reinsertion and citizenship centers" to help identify potential jihadists and prevent extremists from radicalizing them.

LEARN TO TRUST

The final and most important lesson is that countries must build partnerships based on earned trust. On the national level, policymakers should reexamine the relationships between police and intelligence agencies, between external and internal security and intelligence services, between civilian and military services, and between government agencies and the private sector, looking to build trust wherever possible, by arranging more cross-postings, for example.

Investing more in digital intelligence should be a priority.

On the international level, European governments need to earn the trust of partners inside and outside the EU to protect sensitive intelligence that can lead to shared leads and joint operations. And they need to establish good relationships with the U.S. technology companies that may hold data vital to stopping future attacks. To do so, they should negotiate bilateral agreements with the United States that provide the necessary legal safeguards for companies to respond to legitimate requests without breaking U.S. law. EU governments should also consider revising their data-retention laws. An insistence, for privacy reasons, on short data-retention periods has hindered prosecutions in the past.

Investing more in digital intelligence should be a priority. Intelligence professionals understand the value of having bulk access to Internet communications (between Syria and Europe, for example), being able to hack the devices used by terrorists and criminals, and using data-mining techniques to identify suspects. In 2010, for example, British authorities foiled the plans of a group of jihadists to bomb the London Stock Exchange by uncovering their electronic communications. But the revelations of U.S. and British government electronic surveillance programs by the former National Security Agency contractor Edward Snowden have diminished public trust in the use of such techniques. It is essential to rebuild confidence across Europe in the use of these methods—under strict legal safeguards and with independent oversight. Leaders should acknowledge the important role that intelligence agencies play and defend their methods as essential to public safety. To get smaller states on board, the larger powers, such as the United Kingdom and France, should reach out to them to offer support and training. The Club de Berne, a non-EU body where the heads of the internal intelligence services of the EU countries, Norway, and Switzerland meet regularly and oversee the Counter Terrorist Group, which liaises with the EU, would be a good forum for coordinating such efforts.

BREXIT BLUES?

The United Kingdom's vote to leave the EU, or Brexit, has introduced great uncertainty for at least the next two years over the United Kingdom's relationship with Europe. The United Kingdom is Europe's major intelligence power and has long benefited from its close coordination with the United States on security and intelligence gathering. It remains at the cutting edge of digital intelligence—it has around 5,500 people working in this area, compared with France's 2,800 and Germany's 1,000. At the moment, the United Kingdom enjoys excellent bilateral and multilateral relationships with other European intelligence services. That should continue, but politicians will need to show steady nerves to ensure that the security needs of Europe as a whole are placed above the political interests of its individual leaders.

Policymakers must be prepared to cooperate internationally through informal networks, rather than waste time dreaming of new EU institutions, such as a European CIA or FBI. An effective international network could develop among counterterrorism centers, for example, especially to share threat assessments (preferably based on an agreed set of warning levels). The various European national intelligence coordinators, working with the U.S. director of national intelligence, could form another such network. And the United Kingdom will remain a major player in the Club de Berne. Intelligence and security professionals across Europe sincerely hope that the United Kingdom will remain fully engaged, even as they understandably regret the wider disruption that Brexit will cause.

The EU has done much to foster police and judicial cooperation while safeguarding fundamental rights. The common European Arrest Warrant speeds up the extradition of suspects between EU member states, a mechanism the United Kingdom used to return a suspected terrorist to Italy to face trial after the second wave of attempted attacks on London in 2005. Europol provides a valuable avenue through which police can liaise with one another. The Schengen Information System II allows police to share information about suspects, and the Schengen III information-sharing arrangements provide a network for sharing DNA, fingerprints, and vehicle registration databases (the United Kingdom had recently joined this network, but after Brexit, it will have to negotiate a new agreement). Policymakers will now need to put in place arrangements to ensure continued cooperation on law enforcement once the United Kingdom withdraws from the EU.

Close British-EU cooperation should not get in the way of creating a wider network of states, including the United Kingdom, to improve intelligence gathering on terrorist and criminal organizations within and outside Europe's borders. But it will take good statesmanship on all sides to navigate the tough negotiations over the United Kingdom's new relationship with the EU, while creating more powerful, mutually beneficial networks for intelligence sharing and security cooperation across Europe and beyond.

European countries were slow to respond to the rise of ISIS. But they now have the opportunity to override old prejudices, reexamine their counterterrorism strategies, and invest in modern intelligence methods. Even those states that justifiably pride themselves on their police and their ability to access and analyze intelligence can learn from recent events.

Above all, the goal should be to maintain normality—and to increase the ability to swiftly restore it when necessary. This will deprive terrorists of what they seek most: to stoke public fear and disrupt the everyday life of free and democratic societies. They must not be allowed to succeed.

David Omand is a Visiting Professor in the Department of War Studies at King's College London and at Sciences Po, in Paris. He served as the United Kingdom's Security and Intelligence Coordinator from 2002 to 2005.

© Foreign Affairs

German Inefficiency

The Continent's Leader Needs Intelligence Reform

Guido Steinberg

A German policeman stands in front of the Brandenburg Gate on New Year's Eve, 2016.

On December 19, 2016, Germany was hit by its first major Islamist terrorist attack, when Anis Amri, a Tunisian supporter of the Islamic State (ISIS), drove a trailer truck into a Berlin Christmas market, killing 12 and wounding 53. The attack, right in the center of former West Berlin, triggered a heated and nervous debate about how Germany should respond—a debate whose outcome will likely affect the parliamentary elections in September 2017. Many Germans are terrified by law enforcement's failures in the run-up to the attack, and are demanding quick and decisive changes to the country's domestic security architecture. Meanwhile, the complacency of politicians in Berlin and in most of the powerful states—with the notable exception of Bavaria—indicates that they do not seem to have grasped that the system must be completely overhauled if Germany is to be saved from the twin dangers of right-wing populism and jihadist terrorism. If Berlin continues on its current path, electoral catastrophes—and more terrorist attacks—are very likely to rattle Germany in the coming months.

WHISTLING PAST THE GRAVEYARD

Germany has known about the threat of jihadist terror since 2007, when an early warning by the U.S. National Security Agency (NSA) allowed German authorities to foil the plot of the "Sauerland group," whose three members, part of the al Qaeda-affiliated Islamic Jihad Group, planned to perpetrate attacks on targets such as the U.S. Air Force's Ramstein air base. At the time, Germany had a far smaller terrorist scene than its western neighbors France and the United Kingdom, where cells of jihadists from former colonies in North Africa and South Asia had begun to coalesce more than a decade earlier. Part of the reason was that the majority of Germany's Muslims are of Turkish origin, and so have adopted jihadist thought belatedly and in much smaller numbers than those from the Arab world.

But despite this early advantage, the number of German Muslims leaving the country to fight in South Asia and the Middle East rose steadily throughout the 2000s, so that in 2010, Germans formed the largest contingent of Western jihadists in Pakistan. Some German members of al Qaeda even traveled back to their home country with the intention of carrying out attacks, but the CIA and NSA again helped to track the returnees and expose their plots, most notably that of the Duesseldorf cell in 2011. After a short lull in the early 2010s, when it seemed that the jihadist threat might subside, the war in Syria and the emergence of ISIS heightened the appeal of jihad to young Germans. Although many were first drawn to Syria by their desire to help fellow Sunni Muslims in their struggle against Bashar al-Assad, the allure of an Islamic state, which promised life under the rules of sharia, soon provided more sacred motives. By early 2017, some 900 Germans had left their country to live and die in Syria and Iraq.

The number of German Muslims leaving the country to fight in South Asia and the Middle East rose steadily throughout the 2000s, so that in 2010, Germans formed the largest contingent of Western jihadists in Pakistan.

It was long thought in Germany that, just like in other countries, the returnees from Syria would pose the gravest challenges to domestic security. But although this proved to be the case in France and Belgium, most of the jihadists who plotted attacks in Germany in 2016 were Arabs and Berbers from Syria and North Africa, who had first come to Europe in 2014 and 2015. They had arrived with the immense flow of refugees which had started in 2014, and had then flooded Western Europe after the decision of German Chancellor Angela Merkel in September 2015 to open the borders to everyone arriving via the overland Balkan route. ISIS used this golden opportunity to send seasoned personnel to perpetrate attacks, such as the one in France in November 2015, and to prepare for more in Belgium and Germany. It also took advantage of the new recruitment pool in Germany, convincing numerous refugees to attack the country that had granted them asylum. This resulted in several foiled plots and a wave of smaller attacks by ISIS supporters, which preceded the events in Berlin.

STURM UND DRAGNET

The deeper problem is that Germany has virtually outsourced its signals intelligence collection to the United States. This is the result of a deep-rooted German mistrust of intelligence services—a legacy of the country's experiences in the twentieth century with the Nazi Gestapo and the East German Stasi. Even after the attacks of September 11, 2001, successive German governments neglected their own intelligence agencies, leaving the country's national security to allies. While U.S. agencies attempted to find terrorists, the Germans were, by and large, reduced to monitoring people who had already been identified as possible threats. The thus lacked the capability to identify transnational threats originating in the Middle East or South Asia.

A closer examination of the plots of 2016 reveals the extent of this reliance. When the CIA and NSA provided their German colleagues with information about planned attacks, the Germans foiled them. But when the United States had no information, the Germans had to rely on sheer luck and the incompetence of the prospective terrorists to escape from harm. For instance, the Americans provided the Germans with intelligence that Syrian ISIS member Jaber al-Bakr was planning an attack on Berlin-Tegel airport, and German authorities were able to arrest him in Leipzig in October 2016. Other times, however, the Germans were left without a clue, as in the case of Muhammad Daleel, a Syrian ISIS member from Aleppo who tried to blow up a music festival in Ansbach in July 2016, but failed to ignite the deadlier part of his bomb.

A woman stands near a memorial for the victims of the Berlin Christmas market attack, December 2016.

The main difference between the situation now and that before 2015 is that today, after the refugee crisis, neither the United States nor its European partners can cope with the scale of the threat. This had already become obvious after the November 2015 attacks on the Bataclan in Paris. The perpetrators had constantly communicated with each other and with ISIS commanders back in Syria and Iraq, all without the NSA and its European partners being able to monitor the messages due to the effectiveness of modern encryption technology. Some years before, it would have been far more difficult to plan such an attack without tipping off the NSA, but now, with the rapidly rising numbers of jihadists in Europe, the increased professionalism of ISIS' planning, and cheap and easily available technologies, the terrorists have the advantage.

Yet the failure of German security and intelligence agencies is still the heart of the matter, as is brutally revealed by the case of Anis Amri. The Tunisian had been categorized as a potential terrorist since February 2016, but in what amounted to a total security breakdown (involving not only intelligence but also police services), he was neither deported nor arrested after his application for asylum had been rejected. Although he was well-connected to German ISIS supporters, and in spite of reports that he had talked about perpetrating an attack, surveillance of Amri was stopped in September 2016.

REBUILDING THE RECHTSTAAT

Following the attack in Berlin, the government has reacted with a string of measures, including allowing the authorities to monitor potential terrorists with electronic bracelets and to arrest rejected asylum seekers deemed to represent security threats. Although these are necessary reactions to the Berlin attack, they come years too late. Instead, Germany's domestic security system needs a complete overhaul in order to prepare for the terrorist threats of the coming years.

Germany's domestic security system needs a complete overhaul in order to prepare for the terrorist threats of the coming years.

The overhaul will have to start by centralizing the 38 institutions designed to counter jihadist terrorism in Germany. Every state has its own intelligence service and state office of criminal investigation, some of them stronger (such as those in Bavaria), many of them weaker (such as those in Berlin). Their lack of cooperation—and professionalism—led to some of the chaos in the Amri case. Going forward, both intelligence and police will have to work under the direction of their federal colleagues in the Office for the Protection of the Constitution (BfV) and the Federal Criminal Police Office (BKA) if their performance is to improve.

Germany will have to strengthen its intelligence services as well. The increasing number of cases in which terrorists in Germany have been able to secretly communicate with each other and with comrades abroad is alarming, especially because those behind many of the recent attacks in Europe were able to communicate with their superiors in the Middle East for weeks or even months. The German agencies should improve their technical capabilities in the years to come, and the government will have to provide them with the legal basis to do their work. They will never come close to the broad reach and the effectiveness of the NSA, but the failures of 2016 show they must start to get better.

Germany will also have to reestablish control over its borders. Although the number of newly arrived refugees dropped to some 280,000 in 2016, this is the result of states along the Balkan route closing their borders to asylum seekers and the new Turkish policy of stopping migrants from crossing the Aegean Sea. The number of refugees coming from North Africa to Italy via the Mediterranean, and thence northward, is increasing and may rise quickly at any time. Communication among the Schengen member states, moreover, is sorely lacking, and German authorities currently do not know who is entering other European states.

For the time being, it remains unlikely that anything close to these reform steps will be implemented, because even a very basic proposal to centralize the security authorities has met with stiff opposition. This happened when the federal Minister of the Interior, Thomas de Maizière, proposed a similar but more limited step in January 2017, and the state interior ministers outright rejected it. Rather, a meaningful reform of the German security architecture will require a shift in the political culture of the country, which will only be the result of a major change in the political system. This, in turn, could be brought about by a stronger-than-expected performance of right-wing populists in the elections, or by a further series of attacks. Unfortunately, however, it seems that without such a push, the German political elite will remain mired in complacency.

GUIDO STEINBERG is a Senior Associate at the German Institute for International and Security Affairs.

© Foreign Affairs

British Counterterrorism Policy After Westminster

London Can Do More to Prevent Radicalization

Robin Simcox

Floral tributes are attached to railings in Parliament Square following the attack in Westminster, central London, March 2017.

It was always a matter of when, and not if, the United Kingdom was going to suffer another terrorist attack. The death toll from the strike in Westminster stands at four, with dozens more injured. The perpetrator was Khalid Masood, a British citizen and convert to Islam. The Islamic State (also known as ISIS) has released a statement describing Masood as "an Islamic State soldier" who "carried out the operation in response to calls to target citizens of the coalition."

The United Kingdom has long been a target for Islamist extremists. The July 2005 bombings targeting the London transport network (which killed 52) and the stabbing to death of drummer Lee Rigby in May 2013 are evidence, as are the approximately

850 people who have traveled from the country to Syria to fight for ISIS and other radical groups.

However, this only scratches the surface. In virtually every year since 9/11, the United Kingdom has either thwarted or suffered a major terrorist attack. Many were tied to al Qaeda and had their origins in Pakistan. The fertilizer bomb plot of 2004, the transatlantic liquid bomb plot of 2006, and the Easter bomb plot of 2009 are all such examples. Other attacks had their origins in the Levant. Car bombs and a suicide attack in London and Glasgow in 2007 were carried out by the ISIS's precursor group, al Qaeda in Iraq. Terrorist acts planned from Syria in 2015 forced the United Kingdom to carry out a successful drone strike against one of its own citizens in response, the first time it has ever done so.

AN ASSERTIVE POLICY

In confronting the threat of terrorism, London has been anything but passive. Overseas, it has committed its military to war efforts in Afghanistan, Iraq, and Syria and carried out counterterrorism training in Somalia and Mali.

In confronting the threat of terrorism, London has been anything but passive.

Domestically, there have been 264 convictions in British courts for Islamism-inspired terrorism offenses. The Home Office has developed both a counterterrorism strategy and a counter-extremism strategy. The security services are monitoring over 3,000 people in the United Kingdom who are suspected of being willing to commit attacks. MI5, MI6, GCHQ (the United Kingdom's domestic, foreign, and signals intelligence agencies), and the police work together effectively; the intelligence turf wars that blight other European countries are not nearly as pronounced there.

In 2014, then-Home Secretary (and current Prime Minister) Theresa May was able to push through measures to strip British terror suspects of their citizenship if they were dual nationals or if given reasonable cause to believe they could acquire another nationality. The United Kingdom has also been able to deport some foreign terror suspects (although entrenched opposition from the courts on human rights grounds has been a constant roadblock).

This was part of the reason that, in 2005, the Labour government introduced Control Orders. These were subsequently modified by the coalition government, and were renamed Terrorism Prevention and Investigative Measures (TPIMs) in 2011. TPIMs (and Control Orders beforehand) target terror suspects who cannot be charged or deported, allowing the state to confiscate the suspects' passports, prevent them from associating with certain other suspects or going to certain mosques, stop them from using certain types of electronic devices, and impose a curfew on them.

In the ideological sphere, the counter-radicalization Prevent program, which was introduced by the Labour government in 2003 but only really fleshed out post 2006, aims to "stop people from becoming terrorists or supporting terrorism." Prevent allows local government, the police, schools, universities, prisons, hospitals, and Muslim communities to work together to identify and challenge Islamist extremist ideology (although Prevent focuses on all forms of extremism). One increasingly important part of Prevent is Channel, an intervention process intended to draw individuals away from terrorism. It has had thousands of referrals in the last decade.

The United Kingdom's response to Islamic terrorism has been far from perfect. Yet such measures—as well as the presence of the English Channel, the United Kingdom's decision not to be part of the Schengen Area and its caution in accepting large numbers of refugees—has meant that London has been able to protect itself more effectively than other capitals.

NEXT STEPS

There is more to be done. Masood was already on the British intelligence radar, and so MI5 will be analyzing what more it could have done to prevent the attack and others like it in the future. Despite funding increases, of course, MI5 cannot track all potential attackers. The Head of MI5 has previously stated that they can only "hit the crocodiles nearest the boat" and Masood was not regarded as an imminent threat. No security agency gets it right every time, nor can it be expected to. It is impossible to stop all radicalized individuals who have a desire to kill from renting a car or buying a knife.

Yet there are areas for the government to focus its efforts. For starters, the need to dismantle the so-called caliphate in Iraq and Syria is clear. While retaining its focus on ISIS, the United Kingdom cannot ignore the dangers posed by al Qaeda and its affiliates.

Domestically, there is a clear trend of those with a history of petty or violent crime graduating to acts of terrorism. To this end, the government must prioritize addressing radicalization in prison and preventing the dissemination of extremist literature in these prisons. In addition, authorities have been aware since at least 2001 that terrorists fraudulently use state benefits to fund terrorist activity. It is unacceptable that this still takes place with some regularity.

Although Masood was 52 years old, the reality is that ISIS is focusing on ever younger recruits to carry out attacks in the West and using encrypted messaging apps in order to do so. The British government has to try and make young people resilient to the appeal of this ideology. The education system will be an important part of this response. Although better communication of British values and a broader understanding of British history may be no panacea to radicalism, it is likely to do more good than harm. The government must also must ensure that it works closely with technology firms to diminish the impact of ISIS' online activities; it also needs to ensure GCHQ has the capacity to respond to them.

Ultimately, however, these are peripheral battles as long as Islamism is seen as a viable ideology. It is unfortunate, for example, that the Foreign & Commonwealth Office recently submitted evidence to a U.K. Foreign Affairs Committee examining the Muslim Brotherhood that some forms of Islamism embrace "democratic principles and liberal values." This is the soft bigotry of low expectations. There is no evidence that groups like the Muslim Brotherhood have any dedication to liberal values as they would be commonly understood in the West. Indeed, genuine liberals are sidelined due to the perception that they are not "credible voices."

Perhaps Masood's attack will contribute to a change in attitude in the United Kingdom. It should. Only a robust, uncompromising response across the board to the dangers of Islamist ideology—from the state, media, and wider civil society—can ensure that the latest bloodshed in London is not a harbinger of worse to come in the future.

ROBIN SIMCOX is Margaret Thatcher Fellow at the Heritage Foundation.

Europe's Populist Surge

A Long Time in the Making

Cas Mudde

To Viktor go the spoils: Orban at an Austria-Hungary soccer match, June 2016.

The year 2015 was a dreadful one for Europe in general and for the EU in particular. It started with the terrorist attack against the magazine Charlie Hebdo in Paris and ended with an even more deadly jihadist assault in the same city. In between, the EU battled an economic crisis in Greece, which threatened the entire eurozone, and endured a staggering inflow of refugees from the Middle East and other war-torn regions.

The year 2016 has not been much better. More terrorist attacks have shaken the continent. The refugee crisis has abated slightly, but only because the EU has outsourced the problem to Turkey—a country that is itself experiencing a bout of instability. And for the first time, the EU is set to lose a member, the United Kingdom, as a result of the so-called Brexit referendum.

All these developments have helped push populist movements to the center of European politics. The threat of terrorism and anxiety about a massive wave of immigrants from the Muslim world, coupled with the widespread belief that the EU hinders rather than helps when it comes to such problems, have created a perfect storm for populists, especially enhancing the standing of right-wing populists in many countries. Chief among them is Hungarian Prime Minister Viktor Orban, who has taken advantage of public fears to rally opposition to German Chancellor Angela Merkel and her belief that Europe should embrace a Willkommenskultur, a "culture of welcoming." Meanwhile, the eurozone crisis has aided the rise of left-wing, anti-austerity populists in Greece and Spain.

But although the threats to security and economic stability that have rattled Europe in the past few years may have spurred the current populist surge, they did not create it. Its origins lie further back, in the structural shifts in European society and politics that began in the 1960s. Because so much commentary on contemporary populism overlooks its deep historical sources, many observers fail to appreciate the durability of today's populist appeals and the likely staying power of the parties built around them. It's true that populists have often struggled to hold on to power once they've obtained it. But today's social, political, and media landscapes in Europe favor populists more than at any time since the end of World War II. To reverse the populist tide, today's floundering, hollowed-out mainstream European parties and the entrenched elites who guide them will have to respond with far more dexterity and creativity than they have shown in recent decades.

THE PURE PEOPLE

As with any "ism," definitions are crucial. A useful one goes like this: populism is an ideology that separates society into two homogeneous and antagonistic groups, "the pure people" and "the corrupt elite," and that holds that politics should be an expression of "the general will" of the people. With a few exceptions, that kind of thinking remained on the margins of European politics throughout the nineteenth century and much of the twentieth century. Aspects of populism could be found in the communist and fascist movements, particularly during their oppositional phases. But both of those ideologies (and the regimes that embraced them) were essentially elitist, placing a small group of powerful insiders above the masses.

Leader of the Law and Justice party Jaroslaw Kaczynski delivers a speech in Warsaw, Poland, May 2016.

In the first decades of the postwar era, Western European politics was defined by a broad consensus on three key issues: alignment with the United States in the Cold War, the need for more political integration on the continent, and the benefits of maintaining a strong welfare state. Deep and wide support for those positions left little space for ideological alternatives, and populism was no exception. It wasn't until the 1980s that populist thinking truly began to make its mark, with the arrival of radical right-wing parties such as France's National Front, which rose to prominence in the wake of mass immigration and growing unemployment by promising to return France to the monocultural glory of its past.

Today, populist parties are represented in the parliaments of most European countries. The majority are right wing, although not all are radical. Others are left wing or espouse idiosyncratic platforms that are difficult to place on a left-right spectrum: for example, the Italian Five Star Movement, which has found success with a combination of environmentalism, anticorruption rectitude, and antiestablishment rage. In national elections held in the past five years, at least one populist party earned ten percent or more of the vote in 16 European countries. Collectively, populist parties scored an average of 16.5 percent of the vote in those elections, ranging from a staggering 65 percent in Hungary to less than one percent in Luxembourg. Populists now control the largest share of parliamentary seats in six countries: Greece, Hungary, Italy, Poland, Slovakia, and Switzerland. In three of those (Hungary, Italy, and Slovakia), populist parties collectively gained a majority of the votes in the most recent national elections, although in Hungary and Italy the main populist parties are rivals. The situation in Hungary is most striking, where the governing party (Fidesz) and the largest opposition party (Jobbik) are both populist. Finally, in three other countries—Finland, Lithuania, and Norway—populist parties are now part of the governing coalitions.

TINA POLITICS

Most conventional explanations of this trend emphasize the importance of two factors: globalization and the economic crises in Europe that resulted from the financial meltdown of 2008 and the subsequent Great Recession. But the current populist moment is part of a longer story and is rooted in the postindustrial revolution that led to fundamental changes in European societies in the 1960s. During those years, deindustrialization and a steep decline in religious observance weakened the support enjoyed by established center-left and center-right parties, which had been largely dependent on working-class and religious voters. In the quarter century that followed, a gradual realignment in European politics saw voters throw their support to old parties that had become virtually nonideological or to new parties defined by relatively narrow ideological stances.

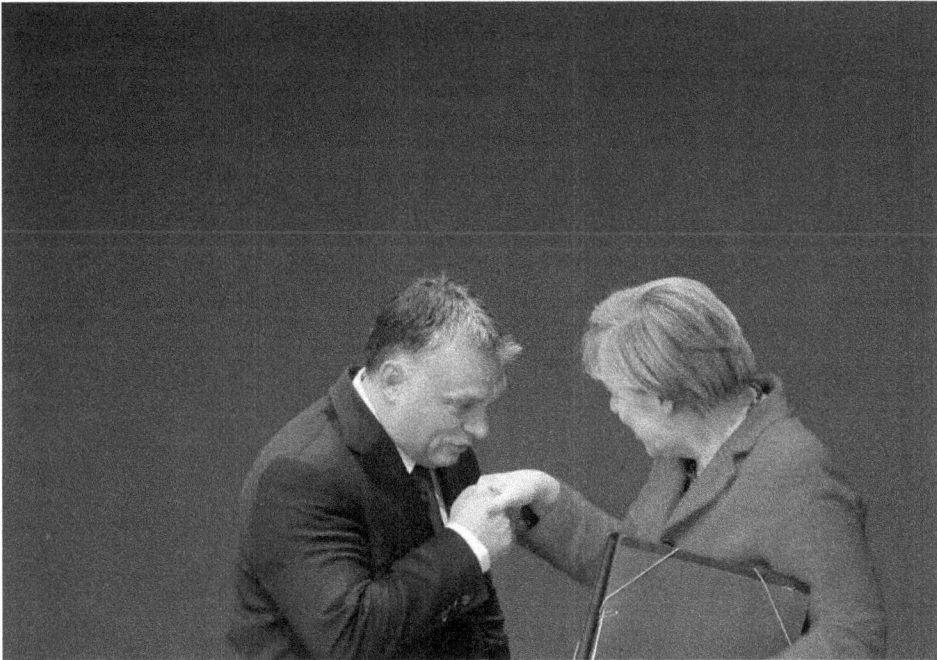

SUSANA VERA / REUTERS

Hungary's Prime Minister Viktor Orban (L) greets German Chancellor Angela Merkel in Madrid, Spain, October 2015.

Later, during the last two decades of the twentieth century, mainstream European parties increasingly converged on a new elite consensus—a common agenda that called for integration through the EU, multiethnic societies, and neoliberal economic reforms. The embrace of a vision of Europe as a cosmopolitan, business-friendly technocracy was particularly pronounced among parties that had traditionally been social democratic, many of which were inspired by British Prime Minister Tony Blair's concept of a "New Labour" party and German Chancellor Gerhard Schröder's move toward a "new center" (neue Mitte). The traditional center-right parties also shifted away from their historical identities, as leaders such as Merkel and David Cameron of the British Conservative Party adopted more centrist and pragmatic approaches to economic and cultural issues.

This convergence created a fertile breeding ground for populism, as many voters began to see political elites as indistinguishable from one another, regardless of their party affiliations. To many Europeans, mainstream elites of all parties also seemed to share an essential powerlessness, owing to two massive transfers of authority that took place in the second half of the twentieth century: from national governments to supranational entities such as the EU and the International Monetary Fund and from democratically elected officials to unelected ones such as central bankers and judges. In many EU member states, vital issues such as border control and monetary policy were no longer the exclusive responsibility of the national government. This led to the emergence of so-called TINA politics—"TINA" being short for "There is no alternative," the line political elites often used as a shorthand for the argument that their responsibility to the EU or the IMF outweighed their duty to be responsive to the demands of voters.

Although populism is not necessarily antidemocratic, it is essentially illiberal.

At the same time, the advent of the Internet produced electorates that were more plugged in to political debates and more independent-minded (although not necessarily better informed), which made them more critical of and less deferential toward traditional elites. In particular, voters became more aware of the fact that elected officials often blamed agents or factors outside their control—the EU, globalization, U.S. policy—for unpopular policies but claimed to be fully in control and took credit whenever policies proved popular.

The Internet also severely limited the gatekeeping function of mainstream media. With far more stories and voices finding an audience, populist narratives—which often contained a whiff of sensationalism or provocation—became particularly attractive to media organizations that were chasing eyeballs as revenue from subscriptions and traditional advertising plummeted. These subtle but profound shifts set the stage for short-term triggers, such as the global financial crisis and the spillover from Middle Eastern conflicts, to turbocharge populism's growth.

POWER HUNGARY

The rise of populism has had important consequences for the state of liberal democracy in Europe. Although populism is not necessarily antidemocratic, it is essentially illiberal, especially in its disregard for minority rights, pluralism, and the rule of law. What is more, as the case of Hungary demonstrates, populism is not merely a campaign strategy or a style of political mobilization that leaders shed as soon as they achieve political power. Since 2010, Orban has openly set about transforming his country into what he described in a 2014 speech as "an illiberal new state based on national foundations," in which the government purposely marginalizes opposition forces by weakening existing state institutions (including the courts) and creating new, largely autonomous governing bodies and packing them with Fidesz loyalists.

There is no reason to anticipate that populism will fade in the near future.

Although the situation in Hungary is exceptional, Orban's success has inspired and emboldened many other right-wing populists in the EU, from Marine Le Pen in France to Jaroslaw Kaczynski in Poland. Most distressing, the rise of populist illiberalism is facing less and less opposition from embattled mainstream parties, which have fallen silent or have even applauded the trend.

Left-wing populists have been nowhere near as successful as their right-wing counterparts. In Greece in 2015, Syriza's amateurish attempt to challenge EU-imposed austerity policies backfired, and Prime Minister Alexis Tsipras was ultimately forced to accept precisely the kinds of spending cuts and structural reforms that he had pledged to prevent. Since then, no other left-wing populist parties have managed to succeed at the national level, with the exception of Podemos (We Can) in Spain. And although left-wing populists are generally less exclusionary than their right-wing counterparts, political polarization in Greece has increased significantly since Syriza came to power in January 2015. Many opponents of the government feel vilified by official rhetoric portraying them as members of a fifth column doing the bidding of Berlin or Brussels. And Tsipras has proposed several laws that could limit the space for political opposition by increasing state control of education and the media.

Marine Le Pen, French National Front leader, campaigns in Paris, France, December 2015.

Even in countries without populist governments, a populist Zeitgeist has taken hold. In many cases, populists now set the agenda and dominate public debate, while mainstream politicians merely react, sometimes even adopting elements of populist rhetoric, peppering their speeches with references to "the people" and condemnations of "elites." Consequently, even traditionally pro-European Christian democrats and social democrats now use "Brussels" as a derogatory term, evoking a distant elite, removed from the concerns of the common people and posing a threat to national sovereignty.

A NEW POPULIST ERA?

Many scholars contend that European populism is an episodic phenomenon—that it creates moments rather than eras—and that although populists can succeed in opposition, they inevitably fail once in power. That is wishful thinking, and those who engage in it generally put too much stock in a few high-profile populist implosions. This sanguine view overlooks the fact that Orban has been in power for six years and still leads the most popular party in Hungary and populism has dominated politics in Slovakia ever since the fall of communism. Meanwhile, Austria is poised to become the first European country in the postwar era to directly elect a populist radical-right president: Norbert Hofer of the Freedom Party, who leads in the most recent opinion polls.

Deep structural changes in European societies produced the current populist wave. Those changes are not likely to be reversed anytime soon, so there is no reason to anticipate that populism will fade in the near future. Moreover, populist parties are growing just as major establishment parties are becoming increasingly obsolete: in many European countries, it has become rare for any party to win more than one-third of the national vote.

Populist parties are ultimately subject to the same basic political laws that constrain their establishment rivals.

Mainstream parties have to develop short-term and long-term strategies to deal with the new reality of fragmented party systems that include influential populist parties. So-called cordons sanitaires—coalition governments, such as that in Belgium, that explicitly seek to exclude populist parties—will become increasingly difficult to sustain. In the many countries where populists now represent the third-or second-biggest party, a cordon sanitaire would force all the other parties to govern together, which would have the unintentional effect of recreating many of the very conditions that led to the rise of European populism in the first place. At the same time, it will become harder for establishment parties to govern alongside populist parties. In recent years, populist parties have been willing to serve as junior partners in coalitions. Now, however, many populist parties are much bigger than their potential mainstream partners and will be far less likely to take a back seat.

Still, populist parties are ultimately subject to the same basic political laws that constrain their establishment rivals. Once they achieve power, they, too, must choose between responsiveness and responsibility—between doing what their voters want and what economic reality and EU institutions dictate. Orban has so far been successful at doing both things at the same time, in part by saying different things to different audiences. But Tsipras has learned about the pressures of responsibility the hard way, and has suffered a significant drop in popularity.

This dilemma for populists presents opportunities for liberal democratic parties, be they new or old, but only if they do not simply attack the populist vision but also provide clear and coherent alternatives. Some establishment figures seem to grasp this. For example, in positioning himself for next year's national elections in France, the center-right politician Alain Juppé has cast himself as "a prophet of happiness" with a positive vision of a more harmonious country—a stark contrast to the negativity and fear-mongering of his rival within the Republicans, Nicolas Sarkozy, and a rebuke to the divisive rhetoric of Le Pen, the right-wing populist leader of the National Front. And in Germany, Merkel has mostly avoided a strong populist backlash—despite immense frustration and pushback inside and outside her own party—by acknowledging public anger while sticking to a clear policy agenda and a positive message: "Wir schaffen das" (We can do this).

In essence, the populist surge is an illiberal democratic response to decades of undemocratic liberal policies. To stem the populist tide, establishment politicians will have to heed the call to repoliticize the crucial issues of the twenty-first century, such as immigration, neoliberal economics, and European integration, bringing them back into the electoral realm and offering coherent and consistent alternatives to the often shortsighted and simplistic offerings of the populists.

CAS MUDDE is an Associate Professor at the School of Public and International Affairs at the University of Georgia and a Researcher at the Center for Research on Extremism at the University of Oslo. Follow him on Twitter @CasMudde.

Merkel's Last Stand

Letter from Berlin

Paul Hockenos

German Chancellor Angela Merkel in Berlin, November 2015.

At first glance, Germany's upcoming national election in late September looks much like those of past years. So far, the issues that will shape the contest appear to be standard fare, and thus overwhelmingly domestic: the German economy, security, migration, and jobs. The leading mainstream parties, the Christian Democratic Union (CDU) and the Social Democratic Party (SPD), aren't that far apart from each other on any of those topics, nor are they on foreign policy. All signs point to a resumption of the ruling CDU–SPD grand coalition, led by Angela Merkel as fourth-term chancellor.

Yet much more is at stake in the German vote—and in the campaign—than initially meets the eye. The politicking will transpire against the background of a European Union sinking further into its deepest crisis since its founding. The wounds of the eurocrisis remain raw. Unpredictable, autocratic leaders in Russia and Turkey are stoking conflicts on Europe's periphery and, in the case of Russian President Vladimir Putin, attempting to sabotage the EU. Exacerbating it all, Donald Trump, the new U.S. president, is shaking the foundations of the Atlantic alliance and has poured fuel on the fire of European right-wing populism.

Germany isn't prepared to take over the leadership of the Atlantic alliance from the United States, much less that of the broader international order that Washington has historically underwritten. But Europe's biggest economy is nevertheless holding the continent together: Berlin, not Brussels, has become the EU's true capital and the guarantor of its stability. Germany's policies reverberate far beyond its borders, and Germany, where the lessons of Nazi rule and World War II are inscribed in the public imagination, remains a bulwark against the illiberal forces tearing Europe apart. With Euroskeptics gaining ground in France and the United Kingdom tied up with Brexit, Germany now stands alone as the guardian of European values—a role it did not seek nor, in many ways, that it is suited for. Every country in Europe has a stake in Germany's election campaign.

MERKEL'S PRINCIPLED STANCE

Europe's extraordinary circumstances are probably one reason why Merkel opted to run for another term, despite having already served as chancellor for nearly 12 years. She remains highly popular, although her principled stance on migration has taken a toll on her support and that of her party. She has no obvious successor as the head of Europe's premier Christian democratic party—and if she were replaced, her CDU successor might well not toe her liberal line on battleground issues, such as migration and Islam's place in Germany, which strays from CDU orthodoxy.

The CDU's arch-conservative Bavarian sister party, the Christian Social Union (CSU), has already waded into populist waters, blasting Merkel's refugee policies in terms that echo and legitimize the stance of the far-right populist Alternative for Germany, or AfD. For the election campaign, though, Merkel has the CSU on board and largely mum on the issue.

WOLFGANG RATTAY / REUTERS

Frauke Petry, the leader of the

Alternative for Germany, arrives for a meting in Koblenz, Germany, with the leaders of other European right-wing parties, January 2017.

Merkel wants to be certain that the CDU and CSU don't make the same mistake that Austrian conservatives did decades ago by opening the door to the Freedom Party, the far-right populist party that served as the conservatives' junior coalition partner in Vienna from 2000 to 2004 and nearly captured Austria's presidency late last year. (Elsewhere in Europe, in countries such as Denmark, Italy, Poland, and Slovakia, far-right groups have also shared in power as formal or informal coalition partners.) Unlike in those countries, none of Germany's parties entertain the possibility of teaming up with the AfD in coalitions, either in the Bundestag or on any other level. But the AfD's almost certain entry into the federal assembly will itself be a seminal event in German politics: the first time since 1949 that a party to the right of the CDU and CSU—one using explicitly racist and nationalistic rhetoric—will win seats in that body. "Nationalist parties may be popping up everywhere now," Norbert Frei, a historian at the University of Jena, wrote in an email. "But in Germany, they're striving to nullify an important element of the Federal Republic's political culture, namely its self-critical engagement with the Nazi past."

The AfD, originally a party of "polite populists" formed to protest the euro and Germany's bailout of indebted southern European states, has in the last few years drifted rightward into volkish nationalism, its ranks filled with lower-middle-class Germans (mostly men) alongside a core of far-right ideologues. It has capitalized on the influx of refugees to survive internal divisions—many of the libertarian-minded academics who opposed the euro in the party's early days have since abandoned it—entering state legislatures across the country and receiving up to 20 percent of the vote in Germany's eastern states. Its leaders endorse Putin and Trump's nationalist, anti-EU positions. The size of the vote the AfD receives in the federal elections will be an important measure of the health of Germany's democracy—and thus of Berlin's ability to hold Europe together.

For now, there's probably a ceiling to the AfD's support. The party "is more radical than Austria's Freedom Party," said Hajo Funke, a German scholar of right-wing extremism. "In its present form, there's no way the AfD is going to tap support from centrist burghers in Germany the way the Freedom Party or the National Front in France do." Funke reckons that the party will garner between 8 and 12 percent of the vote, gaining more only in the event of a successful terrorist attack. Critical to keeping the far right confined, Funke says, is Christian democratic voters' allegiance to Merkel. The CDU remains the country's dominant political party, currently polling at about 33 percent (the Social Democrats are a few points behind). Yet the CDU is considerably weaker than four years ago, when it collected 41.5 percent of the national vote. In state-level votes since then, the party has suffered a string of defeats, as a slice of its voters have peeled off to back the AfD.

CRITICS AND COMPROMISES

As for the campaign's content, "the biggest issues are going to be fought out on the right side of the political spectrum," said Mariam Lau, a columnist for the weekly Die Zeit, referring to migration, but also to the euro, the eurocrisis, security, and relations with Russia. The question is how far Merkel's CDU and the CSU will go to lure voters who might otherwise back the AfD. Will the chancellor make further concessions on migration and integration, as she's done many times before by, for example, imposing a burka ban (she has already proposed one), or will she stand up confidently for her migration policies and a diverse society, as she's done at other times? Will she defend the EU or tactfully distance herself from it? Will she cut Greece slack or keep it pinned to the floor with debt? Will she promote a narrow conception of Germany as a state for German nationals or open it up to non-German nationals, such as people with migration backgrounds? Will she back yet more intense surveillance and policing methods? Much depends on how she approaches these sensitive issues.

The politicking will transpire against the background of a European Union sinking further into its deepest crisis since its founding.

Together with security, migration will be the campaign's most important and divisive issue. The chancellor's position on the refugee influx into Germany has come a long way from the de facto open-door position she took in the summer of 2015, when hundreds of thousands of desperate refugees and migrants where trekking toward Europe. Through a deal with Turkey, tougher legal requirements for refugees, and the refusal to accept asylum applicants from so-called safe states in the Balkans, Germany has cut the rate at which people are entering the country by nearly 75 percent since then. Last week, Merkel took yet another step to appease critics by setting out a wide-ranging plan to more quickly repatriate failed asylum seekers. Nevertheless, she began the year by reminding U.S. President Donald Trump of the Geneva Convention's refugee provisions, a sign that she's determined not to betray Germany's fundamental commitment to the right to asylum.

Merkel's compromises, however, have not placated her critics. Indeed, against fierce pressure from within her own party and from populist challengers, she has resisted closing the border to refugees or capping the number of asylum applicants Germany will accept. She has held firm that all EU countries shoulder asylum seekers according to their size and wealth. And she has approached the right to asylum, in the context of human rights in general, as a pillar of Europe's liberal order, one whose erasure would diminish the continent's democratic credentials and perhaps push more of its states onto the slippery slope of authoritarianism, as has already happened in Hungary and Poland.

FABRIZIO BENSCH / REUTERS

Sigmar Gabriel, then the German economy minister, and Martin Schulz, then the European Parliament president, at an SPD party congress in Berlin, December 2015.

THE CHALLENGE FROM THE LEFT

Merkel's primary opponent in the election is also an ally—and will probably be her deputy chancellor after the vote. A new arrival in German politics, Martin Schulz is a Social Democrat who, very unusually for a German politician, made his name in the European Parliament, rising to its presidency in 2012. Schulz took an unorthodox path to Brussels: he grew up in a working-class family in a coal-mining region of the Rhineland and, rather than finish high school, opted to play semi-professional soccer and later trained to be a book seller. After joining the SPD, Schulz served for a decade as mayor of a small town along the Dutch border, the most recent office in Germany he has held. Since the mid-1990s, he has moved in the rarified environs of the European Parliament as a face Germans know but not as a politician they've tested. Despite his EU credentials, many Germans consider Schulz a gritty, trade-union-minded advocate for the working class.

There has been a long line of Social Democrats who have tried and failed to stop their party's electoral bleeding in recent decades. Now Schulz is on it, and initial polls show him close on Merkel's heels. Upon Schulz's unexpected nomination, the SPD jumped three points in polling and has continued to climb. Yet Germany's left—the SPD, the Greens, and the Left Party—will likely still fall short of a majority. The CDU has only the SPD with which it can form a government, unless it forms a coalition with two parties—say, the Greens and the liberal Free Democratic Party.

In addition to contesting each other and countering the far-right, Merkel and Schulz will have to convince Germans that the EU has a viable future. If the Germans give up on it, Europe's destiny is up for grabs. Trump's proclamations on NATO and Putin's provocations in Eastern Europe have believers in the European project scrambling to beef up the EU's defense and security capabilities, rethink its foreign policy, create a single military command, and, in general, prepare for a life without their strongest ally. Yet neither Schulz nor Merkel appear to have a big-frame vision for the EU's future that he or she can sell to German voters. And ultimately, they have to sell the EU beyond Germany, to the rest of Europe. Germany's dominance in the union has grown since the eurocrisis, and Berlin is often seen as promoting its own interests to the detriment of the union's other members. Certainly, measures such as tempering Germany's record trade surpluses or investing them to help buoy economies outside of Germany would be a step in the right direction. Germany can't rally Europe while appearing to use the EU as a vehicle for its own interests—a criticism that Trump has made and many smaller EU countries have echoed.

A number of events between now and September could upend this fragile calculus. A National Front victory in France's upcoming presidential elections, routs of the CDU in North Rhine-Westphalia, Saarland, or Schleswig-Holstein in state contests, a terrorist attack, renewed trails of refugees, a major escalation in Ukraine, or the CSU's defection from the CDU could cause Merkel and her party to sink in the polls. A Merkel-and-Schulz-led administration isn't a bad option for Germany. If they end up governing together, both must be aware that the fate of Europe rests on their shoulders.

PAUL HOCKENOS is a Berlin-based writer and the author of the forthcoming *Berlin Calling: A Story of Anarchy, Music, the Wall, and the Birth of the New Berlin*.

© Foreign Affairs

There Is No Alternative

Why Germany's Right-Wing Populists Are Losing Steam

Michael Bröning

AfD leader Frauke Petry posing with Heinz-Christian Strache, the head of the Austrian Freedom Party, on the Zugspitze, Germany's highest mountain, near Garmisch-Partenkirchen, June 2016.

In late January, the future looked bright for the Alternative für Deutschland (AfD). Frauke Petry, the party's chief, had gathered Europe's right-wing populists for a summit in the German city of Koblenz, where she appeared on stage with the other leaders of the continent's populist revolt. To the cheering of the crowd, French presidential candidate and National Front head Marine Le Pen declared that, in 2017, "the people of continental Europe will wake up."

In Germany, voters do appear to be waking up—but not in the way that Le Pen envisioned. The AfD has lost around one-third of its popular support since January, according to recent polls. If elections were held today, the party would win between 8 and 11 percent of the vote—a steep decline from the 15 percent it registered last December, following a series of successes in regional elections in 2016. This rapid fall from favor stands in stark contrast to the surge in public support that right-wing populists are enjoying elsewhere in Europe, notably in France and the Netherlands. In the midst of a far-reaching populist revolt, Germany has emerged as an exception—at least for now.

Workers during a warning strike at an Audi factory in Ingolstadt, Germany, November 2008.

PETRYFIED

Three structural dynamics have fueled the AfD's crisis, and each promises to be influential beyond the immediate future. The first is the German government's assumption of tougher migration policies. The political steps that Berlin has taken since July 2015 have been controversial, but they have also significantly reduced the number of refugees arriving in Germany. The refugee deal with Turkey and Berlin's attempts to conclude similar agreements with North African countries such as Egypt, Libya, and Tunisia have effectively robbed the AfD of what was once one of the party's unique selling points: its promise to reduce migrant and refugee inflows. At least for now, Berlin's measures have largely defused what was long predicted to be the determining factor in the federal elections in September.

European populists have won the blue-collar vote by embracing redistributive policies. This has not happened in Germany.

Next, the rise of Martin Schulz as the Social Democratic Party's candidate for the chancellorship has reintroduced the possibility of change to Germany's dormant political center, sapping the AfD of some of its support. A former president of the European Parliament, Schulz has electrified the SPD's base by branding himself as a quintessential pro-European and a counterweight to U.S. President Donald Trump. Schulz has used his pedigree as a political outsider—he has never held elected office in Germany at the national level—to attract dissatisfied and disenfranchised voters, including left-and right-wing populists who regard him as an alternative to the AfD, the Greens, and the far-left Die Linke. By doing so, he has managed to level the playing field with German Chancellor Angela Merkel and has even pulled ahead of her in several national polls, in a remarkably rapid surge.

Finally, the AfD has undermined its own electability by exposing some of its internal contradictions to the public. Since the party's founding in 2013, it has attempted to balance carefully scripted political provocations with attempts to uphold the appearance of conservative respectability. This approach has been central to the party's appeal, attracting center-right voters unhappy with the status quo but reluctant to embrace extremist positions. In recent months, however, this strategic ambiguity has crumbled. At an AfD meeting in mid-January, Björn Höcke, a former history teacher and one of the party's regional leaders, caused an uproar by challenging what he described as Germany's "shameful" approach to its Nazi-era past. "We need nothing less than a 180-degree change of course in our political approach to history," Höcke said. His comments laid an axe to a foundational consensus in German politics, called into question the party's compatibility with a cornerstone of Germany's postwar identity, and alienated some of the AfD's more centrist supporters. Even Petry felt compelled to rebuke Höcke's remarks; she is now struggling to push him out of the party.

But Germany's relationship with its past is hardly the only issue that separates the AfD from the majority of voters. Equally divisive is the party's economic outlook. Other European right-wing populist parties have won the blue-collar vote by embracing redistributive policies. This has not happened in Germany: the AfD still wears the neoliberal robes it donned at its founding during the height of the eurozone crisis. Whereas France's National Front has attracted the working class with promises to lower the retirement age or to increase the minimum wage, the AfD has called for abolishing inheritance and net wealth taxes and for reintroducing bank secrecy, or rules that allow banks to shield information about their clients from the government. Those are hardly positions that win over average Germans.

CHRISTIAN HARTMANN / REUTERS

Martin Schulz in Strasbourg, France, January 2017.

SOVEREIGN IS HE DEFINED BY EXCEPTION?

The AfD's recent decline should remind Europe's political establishment that addressing the root causes of voters' concerns is the single best antidote to populist anger. Germany's efforts to regain control of migration flows without relinquishing its humanitarian principles—as demonstrated by Berlin's commitment to use its G–20 presidency to promote economic development in Africa—is a case in point. The party's fall from favor has also demonstrated the importance of creating real choices in the political mainstream. Offering a viable political alternative to the status quo, as Schulz has, can defuse the anti-establishment appeal of populists. Politicians elsewhere in Europe should take note.

Whether the AfD's apparent collapse will continue is unclear. The refugee deal with Turkey could come apart if tensions between Ankara and Berlin continue to rise; Schulz's appeal to disaffected voters could hit a ceiling; or the Greek economic crisis could reemerge, dividing voters over Berlin's response. Such events would certainly throw a lifeline to the party. On the other hand, the political turmoil of the Trump presidency or further right-wing successes in Europe could undermine the AfD: although right-wing triumphs abroad would galvanize the party's core supporters, they would also encourage an even stronger democratic backlash. Against the backdrop of Europe's populist surge, it would be striking if the country most blemished by extremist fury in the twentieth century were to prove most resistant to its temptations in the twenty first.

MICHAEL BRÖNING is Head of the International Policy Department at the Friedrich-Ebert-Stiftung.

The Schulz Effect Faces Its First Test

Will Reviving Germany's Social Democrats Be Enough to Unseat Merkel?

Alexander Saeedy

Social Democratic Party leader Martin Schulz, Germany, March 1, 2017.

With its new leader Martin Schulz, Germany's center-left Social Democratic Party (SPD) has had a comeback, but it is unclear whether the boost will be enough to unseat Chancellor Angela Merkel in the federal elections in September. According to the most recent German polls, the SPD nudged ahead of Merkel's Christian Democratic Union (CDU) by one percentage point after Schulz was elected to lead at a special party congress on March 19. But on Sunday, voters in Saarland, a small and typically CDU-leaning state in southwestern Germany, seemed not to take heed of the "Schulz surge" as they cast their ballots in regional elections.

Merkel's CDU came in first place with around 40 percent of the vote, while the SPD trailed in second place with just over 29 percent. Although Saarland generally leans conservative, it represents one of the many German heartlands Schulz and the SPD will need to win over if he is to become chancellor this September. Sunday's results in Saarland were certainly disappointing for the SPD, but the elections were admittedly very, very close. Had the German environmentalist Green Party taken more than five percent of the vote in Saarland—they came in at four percent—the SPD's combined forces with far-left Die Linke and the Greens would have given them a so-called red-red-green majority in Saarland, which is precisely the same configuration that Schulz intends to build in the German Bundestag this September.

DE-SCHRÖDERING THE SPD

Since the 1990s, the SPD has been accused of abandoning its working-class roots. The party's most recent chancellor, Gerhard Schröder (who is a very close friend of Vladimir Putin), infamously betrayed the party's socialist ideology in 2003 with his "Agenda 2010," a radical set of reforms that cut unemployment benefits and effectively pushed down the minimum wage. Since then, Merkel's conservative wing has continued to laud Agenda 2010 as a "competitive" economic policy for Germany, while the SPD's hold within the nation's parliament has shrunk to a fraction of its former size.

SPD leaders and supporters alike consider Schulz to be the antidote to the so-called Schröder defect. Much of the SPD's newfound popularity can be attributed to the meteoric rise of Schulz. A humble bookshop owner from Aachen, he served as a local politician for the SPD in the 1980s before joining the European Parliament in Brussels, where he eventually became president in 2012. After stepping down from that position, he was unofficially named the party's candidate for chancellor in January, and ever since, the SPD's support has been on the rise, particularly among younger voters.

At the SPD's special congress near Berlin's Treptower Park last week, Sigmar Gabriel, Germany's Minister of Foreign Affairs and the former governor of the German state of Lower Saxony, acknowledged Schulz's contribution to the party's recent boost in the polls. Speaking to a crowd of over 3,000 SPD members, he openly admitted that the party had struggled to win votes over the last ten years but that "there [was] no need for melancholy. The SPD has a new name, and it's Martin Schulz."

But Schulz remains a relatively unknown figure inside German national politics and lacks the proper list of credentials that usually qualifies candidates for the top spot in German politics. Merkel, for example, holds a doctorate in physics and served as a member of the German Bundestag for 15 years before becoming chancellor. Schulz, for his part, never attended university, and his political experience is limited to a controversial stint as a mayor of a small German town and his tenure in the

European Parliament in Brussels, a body that has long suffered from accusations of non-transparency and disconnectedness with voters.

But in an era where connection to politics as usual is its own kiss of the death, the SPD may be right in assuming that Schulz is the "right man for the right time." He is a welcome break from the typically uninspiring nature of the party's leadership and holds a deeply pro-European stance that is likely to please Germans on the left. Schulz is championing a vision of a "fair Germany" that capitalizes on its past ten years of economic success by rewarding those who have seen their social protections rolled back in the name of "competitiveness." But the big question is: will Germans buy into his vision as well?

THE SCHULZ SURGE

Known on social media as the #SchulzSurge, Schulz has catalyzed support for his once ailing party, largely thanks to his pro-European stance and progressiveness on wage equality and social welfare policies.

"With his biography—he has no final secondary-school examinations and had some problems with alcohol during his youth—his career embodies the social democratic promise of social rise," Michael Roth, Germany's State Minister for European Affairs told me, "His authenticity, his credibility, his admirable rhetorical skills, and his vast experience as a politician are very impressive for all of us."

Among young Germans, there is no better proof of Schulz's popularity than the highly active subreddit dedicated to him, where he has earned the title of "Gottkanzler" (God-Chancellor) among his most devoted followers. Schulz took the time to personally show his gratitude for this community in a January YouTube video, in which he thanked them for their "tremendous support" and for "unleashing a wave that is naturally of great help to me."

"Schulz made the impossible possible," says Tara Hadviger, chair of Jusos Brussels, a Europe-wide grouping for young supporters of Germany's SPD, and a member of the Board of Jusos Aachen, Schulz's home city in Germany. "Young people feel that we actually have a chance of winning against the CDU and Merkel. Thanks to him, the SPD has recently gained more than 13,000 new members, many of whom are young people who believe in his straightforward style as a politician and his support for the EU. He needs to make sure that this momentum keeps on going until the September elections."

Schulz and the SPD are hoping to achieve an "Obama" effect for the German center-left in this year's elections, using the language of social justice and optimism to win young voters who have traditionally seen the SPD as an aged political party when compared with left-leaning counterparts like the German Greens or Die Linke, which was forged from the ashes of East Germany's former Communist Party, the SED.

Although Schulz will only unveil his full vision for an SPD-led chancellery in June, he offered party members a first glance into his platform at Sunday's congress in an hour-long address. The theme of the congress was "Zeit für mehr Gerechtigkeit"—"time for more fairness"—and reflects his notion of an SPD better focused on workers' rights and social justice.

"The well-being of every man, every woman, and every child should stand at the center of our political project," Schulz said at the congress. "If we invest in our future and in the skills of our workers, people will regain faith in our society."

He also called Merkel's cuts to social programs "economically unwise and socially divisive," spoke in favor of free public education, and called the continued gender pay gap "totally unreasonable." Schulz defended the recent introduction of a minimum wage (which was not legally mandated in Germany until 2015) and called for an extended period of benefits for the unemployed, a move that CDU leaders have said would "damage the success" of Germany's historically low unemployment rate, which at 5.9 percent as of February 2017, has touched a 27-year record low.

Jan Techau, Director of the Richard C. Holbrook Forum for Diplomacy at the American Academy of Berlin and former Director of Carnegie Europe, said that Schulz's rebranding of German social democracy was a smart attempt to defend economic liberalism while acknowledging that there were "winners and losers" in economic globalization.

"Schulz's predecessors didn't have a modern interpretation of German social democracy for the global economy and didn't see how the problems of globalization could be used to their benefit, in order to advocate for those who suffer the most from them," he said.

"It's slightly ironic that he's pushing this agenda in a country where the number of losers from globalization isn't tremendously high and where poverty is low. But there's a nagging feeling that something's gone wrong in the German economy, which puts the SPD in the position for some interesting rejuvenation."

FACING OFF AGAINST THE IRON CHANCELLOR

If Schulz takes over the top seat in German politics this autumn, he'll have more on his hands than a boilerplate domestic agenda anchored in workers' rights. He'll also be sharing de facto control of the EU, which stands at an existential crossroads and is grappling with the Gordian knots of Brexit, immigration, an increasingly bellicose and authoritarian Turkey, and the future of the EU itself.

"There are for sure no easy solutions to complex tasks such as completing the European Monetary Union and Brexit," said Roth. "But as the former President of the European Parliament, Martin Schulz understands the complexity of European politics. Importantly, during his final years in Brussels, he learned that no single European country can bring about solutions on his own."

But some wonder whether Schulz's experience in Brussels—and lack of experience in German politics—means that he would prove an amateur chancellor.

"Schulz has no real executive experience besides his tenure as an EU lawmaker in the European Parliament, arguably the most flawed institution inside of Brussels, where it's the norm to take positions that are far away from political reality," said Techau. "Reality doesn't bite you there. As Chancellor, Schulz will have to learn that what you say and what you do cannot be far out of line from each other."

The SPD should also be keen to follow the warnings from recent elections in the Netherlands that the status quo for Europe's center-left is simply unsustainable. There, far-right populists were defeated in recent elections by Mark Rutte's center-right VVD, or the People's Party of Freedom of Democracy, while the Dutch Labor Party (Partij van de Arbeid)—the Dutch sister to the SPD—suffered its worst defeat in recent history, a rumored casualty of a toxic association with neoliberalism and European austerity.

How Schulz will attempt to bridge the historically toxic contradictions of the modern center-left is yet unclear for the German SPD. But he seems prepared to circumvent the method of his British counterpart Jeremy Corbyn, whose redefinition of the British Labour Party has attempted to revitalize the party through a hard-left return to socialism while silently maligning the European Union and its support for economic liberalization.

"Europe lies directly in the best interests of Germany," Schulz intoned at the SPD congress. "The EU was created alongside the spirit of our unified Germany, and we must fight against those who will try to destroy this project."

But the proof of the pudding is in the eating, meaning that Schulz will need to turn his social media buzz into votes. Although the SPD has polled well through the beginning of 2017, he has yet to begin a full-fledged campaign against Merkel, who has successfully defeated Schulz's party in three separate elections, while veering her party more to the left on social policy. This means it may prove hard for Schulz's progressive message to win defectors from the political center.

But his prospects to build a coalition with the German Greens and hard-left Die Linke nonetheless appear strong. And as long as Schulz can continue to enchant the hearts and minds of the German people, Merkel's 12-year tenure over Europe's most powerful nation during some of the continent's most troubled days may very well be coming to an end.

"The new SPD chief is a magician," wrote Christian Stenzel, an editor at Bild, Germany's most-read newspaper, on the night of Schulz's nomination. "He's successfully made his long years in the Eurocrat-Spaceship of Brussels disappear while ensuring his supporters' attention with the promise of free public education." But, Stenzel warned, Schulz's magic may prove ineffective against the chancellor, whose steeliness has sometimes earned her the title of "die eiserne Kanzlerin"—"the iron chancellor," a title historically used to refer to Otto van Bismarck, and which is usually employed to praise Merkel's "tough but fair" approach to international politics.

"Schulz ought to keep a good rabbit in his top hat until the elections," she wrote, "since it will prove difficult to witch Angela Merkel out of the chancellorship."

ALEXANDER SAEEDY is a public policy researcher living in Brussels, Belgium. His work has appeared in Reuters, Vice News, *International Business Times*, and elsewhere.

The Future of Dutch Democracy

What the Election Revealed About the Establishment—and Its Challengers

Cas Mudde

Ducks in Volendam, February 2017.

It must be quiet now in Volendam, a small Dutch fishing town around ten miles northeast of Amsterdam. To most Dutch people, Volendam is an anomaly, a deeply religious place where older residents still wear traditional costumes. To the foreign journalists who descended on Volendam in the weeks before the Netherlands' March 15 parliamentary elections, it represented something else: the Dutch heartland, where disaffected voters were flocking to support Geert Wilders, the leader of the radical-right Party for Freedom (PVV), the Netherlands' most famous politician, and, most important in this story, the Dutch embodiment of the global populist surge that contributed to the Brexit vote and the election of Donald Trump as U.S. president. No matter that Wilders' party never stood a chance of receiving more than a quarter of the vote, thanks in part to the

Netherlands' proportional electoral system and its proliferation of political parties: the Dutch elections were to be the bellwether of the West's political future—the "year's first test for Europe's populists," as The Economist put it.

In the end, the PVV lost royally to Prime Minister Mark Rutte's conservative People's Party for Freedom and Democracy (VVD), which took 21 percent of the vote—one and a half times as much as the PVV's 13 percent. One way to understand that outcome is through a framework developed by the late German-American economist Albert Hirschman. Hirschman used the terms "exit," "voice," and "loyalty" to describe how the members of firms, organizations, and states behave when confronted with problems: they can choose to withdraw from a troubled group, voice their concerns, or stick around. These three kinds of actions have clear analogues in electoral politics. Exit corresponds to nonvoting, voice to voting for protest parties, such as the PVV, and loyalty to continued support for establishment parties. Viewed through this lens, the Dutch elections confirmed some broader trends in the West but also demonstrated a number of exceptions. As in other European countries, voters' loyalty to establishment parties declined sharply, and protest votes increased. In the Netherlands, however, populist parties captured only part of the protest vote, which was fragmented by a range of medium-sized and small parties. What is more, few Dutch voters chose to exit the electoral process—voter turnout was the highest in two decades. And as elsewhere, populism will remain at the center of the Netherlands' politics unless establishment parties address their constituents' concerns in areas beyond the issues of immigration and security.

YVES HERMAN / REUTERS

Dutch Prime Minister Mark Rutte campaigning in The Hague, March 2017.

THE ESTABLISHMENT'S DECLINE AND THE SOCIAL DEMOCRATS' IMPLOSION

In the first few decades of the postwar period, many European countries were ruled by two big parties: a center-right conservative or Christian democratic party and a center-left social democratic party. These centrist parties often alternated in power, sometimes with the support of a smaller party. From Austria to the United Kingdom, they tended to gain the vast majority of their citizens' votes—sometimes up to 90 percent.

Few such dominant centrist parties remain today. Even in Germany, the Christian Democratic Union and the Social Democratic Party together poll at only around two-thirds of the vote. The Dutch party system has always been somewhat fragmented, but in the Netherlands, too, a similar trend has held. In 1986, the country's three leading parties–the Christian Democratic Appeal (CDA), the Labor Party (PvdA), and the VVD–secured 85 percent of the vote. This year, they won a mere 39 percent.

Few dominant centrist parties remain today.

The decline of the Netherlands' establishment parties is primarily the result of the implosion of the country's social democrats—a collapse that has taken place across the continent, in groups from the British Labour Party to the Greek Panhellenic Socialist Movement. That process started in the 1990s, when, faced with declining working classes, most social democratic parties chose to embrace pro-market positions, leaving some of their former constituents to back right-or left-wing populist parties instead. For its part, the Dutch PvdA has been struggling for years to satisfy its shrinking but increasingly heterogeneous base, which includes both Muslim and Islamophobic workers. The party's most recent peak came in 1986, when it received around one-third of the vote. After years of decline, the PvdA bounced back to nearly 25 percent in the elections of 2012, bringing it into government with the VVD. But the PvdA has now paid the price for so eagerly joining the second Rutte government, which voters regarded as a mostly right-wing project, devoid of significant social democratic features. In last month's election, the PvdA's vote share fell by over 19 percentage points, to 5.7 percent, granting the party just nine seats in the parliament's lower house. It was the biggest electoral defeat in Dutch history—so big that one of the PvdA's leading members, the outgoing Minister of the Interior Ronald Plaskerk, suggested that the PvdA merge with the GreenLeft party, which took 14 seats but has never before governed in a ruling coalition, rather than constitute its own parliamentary faction. This seems short-sighted, as the PvdA still seems to have the loyalty of older, not highly educated voters in the north of the country—and that is not exactly the core electorate of GreenLeft, whose supporters tend to be young, highly educated, and urban.

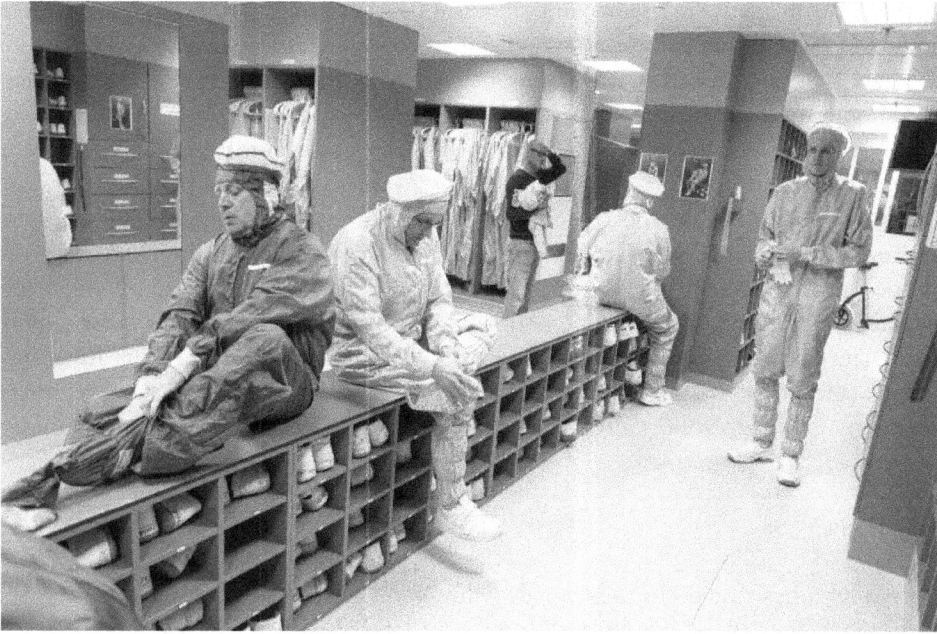

At a factory in Veldhoven, the Netherlands, January 2013.

VOX POPULI

Most foreign observers framed the Dutch elections as a struggle between emboldened populists and an embattled establishment. It is true that, for some time, the VVD and the PVV were neck and neck in the polls. But it is important to recall that populism has been a constant feature of Dutch politics since at least the beginning of the twenty-first century. In the elections of 2002, for example, the right-wing populist List Pim Fortuyn won 17 percent of the vote, taking 26 seats in what was the biggest win by any new party in the postwar era. What is more, support for populist parties has not grown linearly. The PVV, which took 13 percent of the vote last month, received slightly less (10.1 percent) in 2012 and slightly more (15.5 percent) in 2010. In other words, the PVV not only performed far worse than some polls suggested it would—it also did worse than in the last general election.

It is also important to note that protest votes are a product not only of what populists do but also of what other parties offer. The PVV has certainly been undermined by the CDA's and the VVD's moves to the right: the latter two parties made the defense of what they describe as Christian and Dutch institutions and values against the alleged threat posed by Muslims and their naïve secular helpers central to their campaigns. But Dutch voters can choose from 25 other parties, as well, and populist radical-right groups are not the only ones that can give citizens a voice against the status quo. For a while, the radical left Socialist Party filled such a role, but in recent years its platform has become significantly less populist—it now mainly targets right-wing parties rather than all establishment ones—which may explain the party's inability to attract dissatisfied less educated voters. At the same time, some smaller, non-populist antiestablishment parties have emerged, such as the animal-rights Party for the Animals and the pro-immigrant DENK party, which took 3.2 and two percent of the vote, respectively, in this year's elections. What is more, although GreenLeft has been around for decades, since it has never served in government, the support it drew should also be viewed as a kind of protest vote. In short, the Netherlands is home to many protest voices—not just right-wing populist ones. And although the situation is not unique to the Netherlands—for instance, in Spain the new center-right Citizens party has done well, and in Greece the pro-European The River has been a fairly successful newcomer—the Dutch situation stands out for the level of its fragmentation, with almost all established and challenger parties receiving well under fifteen percent of the vote.

NO EXIT?

As for who has exited electoral politics, the Netherlands has always had high voter turnout levels relative to the rest of Europe, at least in parliamentary elections. Since the country abolished compulsory voting in 1970, between 74 and 87 percent of eligible voters have participated in parliamentary elections. This year, just under 81 percent did. Turnout increased among all age groups relative to 2012, except for voters between the ages of 18 and 24, for whom participation rates dropped from 77 to 67 percent. Almost three times as many young people thus chose not to vote as voted for the party that performed best among their peers—the GreenLeft party, which took 12 percent of the youth vote. And whereas 95 percent of highly educated voters over the age of 55 voted, only 48 percent of less educated voters between 18 and 34 did, according to Ipsos, a research group. Because the parties that are mostly likely to form a government have either a relatively old or a highly educated electorate, it is possible that less educated young voters will be further marginalized in the years ahead. Although there are various reasons for the low participation among Dutch youth, the election campaign, which was dominated by issues such as immigration and terrorism, did more to appeal to the fears of the old than the tolerance of the young.

The Netherlands is home to many protest voices—not just right-wing populist ones.

The other form of exit that the recent election demonstrated was the continuing decline in the number of female members of parliament. The Netherlands is widely seen as an emancipated and tolerant country, and for good reason. Despite the dominance of Islamophobia in public discourse, Dutch people are still among the most tolerant in the world in terms of their support for gay rights and gender rights, for example. Yet Dutch politics remain an extremely male-dominated affair. The

Netherlands has never had a female prime minister, nor have its three established parties ever had a female leader. Even the progressive Democrats 66 party—a relative newcomer in the political establishment—has only once been led by a woman, for the 1998 elections. Indeed, of all the medium-sized parties, only GreenLeft holds a decent track record in this respect, having had a female-male joint leadership for the 1994 elections and a female head, Femke Halsema, for the 2003, 2006, and 2010 elections.

It should therefore be no surprise that only four of the 28 parties that contested the 2017 parliamentary elections had a female leader. Only 35 percent of the 1,114 candidates who participated in the election were female, and only 36 percent of the 150 members of the new parliament are women—a small drop from 2012 and a bigger one from 2010. Those figures put the Netherlands above the EU and OECD average, which is 28 percent, and on par with many other northern European countries. Still, the low representation of female politicians could negatively affect legislation, particularly when it comes to so-called women's issues, and the low visibility of female politicians could discourage young women from becoming politically active. The dearth of women in politics also weakens the country's credibility as a global force for women's rights—a role to which consecutive governments have aspired.

Michael Kooren / REUTERS

Members of the Dutch parliament during a meeting in The Hague, March 2017.

STUCK IN THE MIDDLE WITH YOU

The Netherlands has neither defeated nor succumbed to populism. Right-wing populism remains a medium-sized feature of the country's politics, one that influences public debate but is still excluded from government. In this sense, the Netherlands' situation is somewhere between that of France, where the populist radical-right National Front is challenging mainstream parties for the presidency, and that of Germany, where the Alternative for Germany is a small annoyance in a political system still dominated by two relatively big parties. In the Netherlands, as elsewhere, national elections are first and foremost domestic affairs, affected only marginally by global or regional trends.

The challenge for the next Dutch government will be to find a way not just to exclude the populist radical right from power but also to weaken its base. As all the main parties have explicitly said they would not govern with the PVV, the next government will probably be a coalition of the CDA, D66, GreenLeft, and VVD. All of those parties support the basic features of the previous status quo—most notably, European integration, liberal democracy, and a multicultural society—but they have responded very differently to the challenge that the populist radical right poses to them. Whereas D66 and GreenLeft have doubled down on their support for integration, the CDA and VVD have adopted more authoritarian and nativist positions, more regularly giving voice to what might be desscribed as soft euroskepticism and Islamophobia. If the four parties can't find a positively defined compromise, the new government will be perceived mostly as an anti-Wilders coalition, which would keep the PVV and its issues central to Dutch politics.

If the new coalition is able to come together on a positive agenda, that could change. By emphasizing some of the major concerns of the Dutch population that have been pushed to the sidelines by the so-called three Is (immigration, integration, and Islam), the coalition could not just weaken the electoral base of the PVV but also re-energize women and young people, who care more about issues such as education, employment, health care, and the future of the welfare state. All of those concerns relate to the overarching issues of European and ethnocultural integration, and none of them should be reduced to problems of identity and security.

CAS MUDDE is an Associate Professor at the School of Public and International Affairs at the University of Georgia, a Researcher at the Center for Research on Extremism at the University of Oslo, and the author of *On Extremism and Democracy in Europe*. Follow him on Twitter @CasMudde.

Salvaging Brexit

The Right Way to Leave the EU

Swati Dhingra

England expects: in Portsmouth, once a major shipbuilding port, November 2013.

On June 30, a week after the British public voted to leave the EU, Theresa May gave a speech launching her candidacy for prime minister in which she declared, "Brexit means Brexit." Her message was straightforward: even though she herself had supported remaining in the EU, she would not hesitate to implement the will of the voters. Yet months after assuming office, May has yet to answer crucial questions about what a British exit, or Brexit, would mean for trade, immigration, and financial services. It is still not at all obvious what Brexit will actually look like.

That's because the referendum has confronted the government with two distinct but related problems: how to leave the EU as painlessly as possible and how to reverse the years of economic neglect that have divided the country. Solving each will require hard choices, and whatever the politicians decide, some of their supporters will feel let down. With this in mind, they should prioritize prosperity over politics and defy radicals on both sides of the debate. Simply ignoring the referendum result would be politically untenable. But abruptly abandoning the single market, which guarantees the free movement of goods, services, and people, would cause widespread economic hardship.

The best path forward, then, is to strike a temporary deal to keep the United Kingdom in the single market—a deal similar to that which Norway enjoys. Such an arrangement would remove uncertainty among businesses over the United Kingdom's future relations with its biggest trade and investment partner and would buy time to work out a permanent settlement. Assuming it can be sold politically at home, such an interim solution should also prove palatable to the EU.

But trade policy can achieve only so much. In order to respond to the grievances that led to the Brexit vote in the first place, the British government also needs to take big and immediate steps to restore economic equality and raise the country's potential for future growth. To that end, it should rebuild its creaking infrastructure and overstressed public health and educational systems. Only by targeting the underlying sources of economic anxiety can policymakers finally begin to heal a broken nation.

IT'S NOT EU, IT'S ME

TOBY MELVILLE / REUTERS

Nigel Farage celebrates after the Brexit vote, June 2016.

In order to understand why the British people chose to leave the EU, it's necessary to understand what has happened to the British economy in the four decades since the country voted for membership in the European Economic Community. In 1975, two years after it acceded to the EEC, the United Kingdom held a referendum on continued membership. As in this year's vote, those who wanted to leave in 1975 claimed that doing so would lower prices, boost wages, and create jobs for British workers. A majority of the public rejected these claims, and 67 percent of voters chose to remain in the EEC. This time around, obviously, the result was different; only 48 percent opted to stay.

The shift in public opinion can be explained by the intervening increase in economic stress. Although the "leave" campaign's message in 2016 centered on the need to regain British sovereignty, curtail immigration, and stop contributing to the EU budget, many Britons used their votes to express anger at the country's political establishment and its failed economic policies instead. That shouldn't be surprising: even as the economy has grown, the gap between the top and the bottom has stretched wider and wider. In 1980, the top ten percent earned 2.7 times as much as the bottom ten percent; in 2013, the top ten percent took home 3.7 times as much. This is because, for decades, median wage growth has lagged behind average wage growth. In other words, the pie has grown, but workers have seen their slices grow far slower. The financial crisis only made things worse. From 2003 to 2014, all workers suffered as average weekly earnings shrank by 1.8 percent, but the poorest did the worst, as median earnings slid by 2.8 percent over that period. It's not enough to just blame the crisis, however. As far back as 2000, the share of working-age men without qualifications (having left school before the age of 16) who were not active in the labor force had reached 30 percent, compared with less than four percent two decades earlier. By April 2016, that figure stood at over 43 percent.

The British state bears most of the blame for the economic malaise.

The state bears most of the blame for these problems. For years, it has underinvested in public services, eroded the power of trade unions, and failed to promote employment or raise wages. The national minimum wage remained low by international standards for decades, until a Labour government raised it in 1998. The result has been that for many in the United Kingdom, having a job is no guarantee of financial security. Half of poor children in the country have parents who work but are nevertheless below the poverty line.

In recent years, one of the worst examples of government underinvestment has been in health care. In 2010, the new coalition government of Prime Minister David Cameron pledged to protect the National Health Service from austerity.

Despite this guarantee, however, health-care spending has grown by just 1.2 percent per year since 2010, compared with 3.7 percent between 1949 and 1979 and over 6.7 percent from 2007 to 2009, during the financial crisis. The United Kingdom now ranks 13th among the 15 original members of the EU in the percentage of GDP spent on health care. Cuts to the NHS' budget made in the name of efficiency have led to perverse policies, such as hiring expensive temporary staff to meet the shortfall in permanent employees. Remaining staff feel underpaid and overworked.

And it's not just health care where the government has failed. In 2010, the coalition government also reduced child benefits, a policy that researchers at the Institute for Fiscal Studies estimated would push an extra 200,000 children into poverty by 2016. Sure enough, the share of children living in relative poverty ticked up from 27 percent in 2011 to 29 percent in 2015, an increase of 300,000 children, even as the economy recovered.

The imposition of fiscal austerity after 2010 was the coup de grâce for many of the country's most deprived regions. London's poorer boroughs, England's forgotten seaside towns, and the declining industrial areas of northern England, the South Wales Valleys, and Glasgow have experienced the biggest declines in welfare payments over the last six years. In contrast, the more prosperous south and east of England have seen only small spending reductions, since many of the cuts were to public spending that mostly benefited poor individuals. Reductions in disability benefits, housing-support payments, and unemployment assistance hurt most those areas that already had the highest shares of claimants.

DIDN'T WE ALMOST HAVE IT ALL

Real as the anger is, scapegoating the EU for British economic hardship is unfair. In fact, it's doubly so: not only is the British government responsible for the problem, but the EU has actually mitigated its impact. Forty years of data point to the overwhelming conclusion that EU membership reduced the price of goods, increased real wages, and helped fund British public services.

The EU did all this by reducing barriers to trade, which increased competition among firms and caused them to slash the markups they charged consumers. According to a study by the economist Harald Badinger, for example, markups for manufacturing goods across ten EU states fell from 38 percent to 28 percent of costs between 1981 and 1999. What's more, as markets integrated, consumers could more easily purchase products from other countries, which harmonized prices across borders. The economist John Rogers has shown that the local prices of dozens of household goods—from bread to wine to sweaters—converged dramatically between

1990 and 2001. By the end of that period, prices varied within the EU about as much as they did within the United States.

At the same time as the EU lowered prices, it also raised British workers' job prospects, since British businesses expanded production as they obtained cheaper access to European markets. According to researchers at the Institute for Fiscal Studies, this helped raise real wages in the United Kingdom and caused unemployment to fall by 0.7 percentage points between 1988 and 1999. Firms also intensified their research and development to respond to increased competition, which in turn increased overall economic productivity.

Economic hardship, inequality, and political alienation are not unique to the United Kingdom.

Another pillar of the EU, the free movement of people, has driven both economic growth and economic fear. Over the past four decades, workers from the poorer countries of Europe have flocked to the relatively prosperous United Kingdom—over a third of the 8.5 million immigrants currently in the country hail from elsewhere in the EU. Ever since the United Kingdom's accession to the EEC, many voters have feared that these immigrants would displace British workers. This concern played an important role in the June referendum: the higher an area's share of immigrants or the larger its recent increases in immigration, the more likely it was to vote to leave.

Yet immigration from other EU states has not actually harmed British citizens. Even after the EU expanded in the first decade of this century to include much of eastern Europe, there is no evidence that British-born workers experienced higher unemployment or lower wages in counties with above-average numbers of EU immigrants. Nor has EU immigration exacerbated inequality by harming less skilled workers, the segment most vulnerable to competition from immigrants. Changes in wages and joblessness for this group show little correlation with changes in EU immigration.

European immigrants have even been a boon to public finances, because they pay more in taxes than they consume in government services. Euroskeptics often accuse immigrants of robbing British citizens of places in schools and hospitals, but given immigrants' net contributions to such services, these deprivations are more accurately characterized as the result of chronic government underinvestment. Nor have immigrants from the EU undermined social stability: in 2013, researchers at the London School of Economics and University College London found that the large wave of economic immigrants from eastern Europe after the enlargement of the EU in 2004 did not lead to more violent crime or theft.

BREAKING UP IS HARD TO DO

David Cameron leaves an eu leaders summit in Brussels, February 2016.

Despite the benefits of staying in the EU, of course, voters chose to leave it, and now the government must respect their decision. But there are several different forms that the departure could take. The most sensible option would be a deal similar to Norway's, whereby the United Kingdom would remain a member of the single market by joining the European Economic Area, a group of all the EU members and three nonmember countries (Iceland, Liechtenstein, and Norway) that trade freely with the EU but do not participate in its political institutions. Under this arrangement, the costs of trade would still rise, since the United Kingdom would face some nontariff barriers that currently apply to the non-EU members of the EEA. To avoid duties, manufacturers would have to prove that their goods qualified as made in the United Kingdom, for example, a costly process thanks to increasingly complex global supply chains. The European Commission might also impose tariffs on British exports if it ruled that they were being sold to the EU below market price. In 2006, for example, Norwegian salmon exporters who received financial support from the Norwegian government incurred a 16 percent tariff. The United Kingdom would also lose the ability to influence future reductions in trade barriers, such as those the EU is considering in the service sector, which makes up a large part of the British economy. But by preserving access to the single market, this approach would minimize the losses from reduced trade and investment.

Obtaining a Norwegian-style deal wouldn't be easy, however. For one thing, it would require joining the European Free Trade Association—composed of the three non-EU members of the EEA plus Switzerland—which might be unwilling to let the United Kingdom in. Norway has already said it might block British participation, as the relevant agreements have evolved over 20 years to reflect the needs of the association's current members. But Norway's opposition is not certain, and such a deal should prove more palatable to the EU than any other option, since if it were framed as a temporary measure, it would give the union time to think about how it will deal with emerging threats to the European project. The economic hardship, inequality, and political alienation that led to the Brexit vote are not unique to the United Kingdom; they are also present in France, Italy, and the Netherlands, any of which could soon face a similar campaign to leave. The EU must walk a fine line: if it is too soft on the United Kingdom, a host of other countries will want to renegotiate their positions in the EU, but if it is too harsh, it will further alienate anti-EU voters.

Free movement of labor is the sine qua non of the EU.

Perhaps a greater challenge would be getting the British public to accept the continued free movement of EU citizens, sure to be part of any Norwegian-style deal but a redline for many Britons in the leave camp. As a result, some prominent figures, including Rupert Harrison, former chair of the Council of Economic Advisers, have floated the idea of an "EEA minus" option. Such a deal would involve a comprehensive British-EU free-trade agreement similar to the Swiss-EU deal but, crucially, also restrictions on immigration. From the EU's perspective, however, this would be a nonstarter. Free movement of labor is the sine qua non of the EU, and the Swiss had to accept it in order to get deep access to the single market. Even after a referendum in 2014 in which the Swiss people voted to limit immigration from the EU, Brussels refused to let the country impose any limits on movement without losing all of its EU financial and trading rights. Besides, Switzerland's deals with the EU took over 20 years to negotiate, time the United Kingdom can ill afford. And to keep the club together, the EU cannot make leaving too easy.

The only path that would allow the United Kingdom to control immigration and free it from EU regulations and trade policy would be to exit the single market entirely, leaving the country with no comprehensive free-trade agreement with the rest of Europe. Were it to take this route, the United Kingdom would face harsh external tariffs, which, in an ironic twist, would hit hardest some of the areas that voted to leave.

To understand what's at stake, consider the northern industrial city of Sunderland, which voted for Brexit by a 22 percent margin. Sunderland is home to one of Nissan's most cost-efficient manufacturing plants, and last year, it began producing the company's newest luxury car, the Infiniti Q30. About half of British car exports currently go to the EU, which they can enter duty free. Should the United Kingdom leave the EU without a trade deal, it would be treated just like any other non-European trading partner, subject to the default World Trade Organization rules, under which the EU would charge its usual ten percent import tax on cars. No longer so attractive to Nissan, Sunderland could turn into Detroit.

Nissan isn't the only company facing this problem. In a 2014 survey, the Society of Motor Manufacturers and Traders, a British industry group, found that 70 percent of its members expected that leaving the EU would hurt their business in the medium or long term, and three-quarters felt that it would reduce foreign investment in the United Kingdom. History suggests that they're right: the British car industry spent a decade stuck in the slow lane until the country merged with the single market in 1973, allowing British manufacturers to get the same access as French and German ones.

To counter such gloomy predictions, the leave campaign set out grand visions of resuscitating trade within the Commonwealth or reorienting trade toward China or the United States. On the surface, these sound like great ideas, but nothing currently stops the United Kingdom from trading with those countries as a member of the single market. (Indeed, Germany does exactly that, and with great success.) Making up for the loss of membership in the single market would prove difficult, moreover, no matter how ambitious the new trade deals outside the EU were. For one thing, economists have long known that countries trade most with large, rich, nearby markets—and in the case of the United Kingdom, that's the EU. For another thing, trade agreements take many years to negotiate. And without the clout of the EU, British trade negotiators would find it far harder to defend the United Kingdom's interests against those of large countries such as China and the United States.

Besides, with tariffs at record lows, these deals have become less about reducing import duties and more about harmonizing regulations. Many countries outside the EU still lag far behind the United Kingdom in product and labor standards, and so bringing British rules in line with less stringent countries would prove politically difficult and often undesirable. In short, despite what the Brexiteers promised, abandoning the single market would do grave damage to the British economy.

LONDON BRIDGE IS FALLING DOWN

Steelworks in teesside where major job losses were announced in January 2009.

Not only would striking a trade arrangement with the EU soften the blow of leaving; it would also give the United Kingdom the time and resources to get its own house in order. Over the past two decades, the fortunes of the wealthiest Britons have risen, while the poorest have been stuck in a cycle of falling wages and unfulfilling work. Geography has become destiny: London and the prosperous south and east of England feel increasingly like a different country from the declining industrial north. In the referendum, the latter voted as though it were seeking revenge on an elite it felt had forgotten it. Indeed, the lower the wage growth in a given region, the more likely its people were to vote to leave. Unfortunately, such votes were masochistic. The same regions that voted to leave are those that depend the most heavily on EU trade, investment, and transfers. Leave voters were also poorer and less educated than the average—the very group that will suffer more than most if the United Kingdom leaves the EU.

There are promising signs that May and her allies within the Conservative Party have recognized the scale of the problem. Since the vote, they have proposed a number of progressive policies, such as transferring funds from richer regions to poorer ones and giving workers representation on company boards. Although they would help, however, such changes would not go far enough. The United Kingdom needs to make a more fundamental shift away from its neoliberal ideology, which presumes that government efforts to promote growth never work and that balanced budgets are next to godliness, back to its earlier tradition of investing heavily in assets that raise long-term growth. Even the most ardent believers in the free market, including Germany and the United States, support their domestic industries—through public investment in research and development, for example—because they recognize that this kind of spending promotes future growth and economic equality.

Unfortunately, the vote to leave was masochistic.

Nothing illustrates what has gone wrong with the United Kingdom better than education. Today, poor British children perform worse in school than their richer classmates, and the correlation between socioeconomic background and school performance, although present in every rich country, is stronger in the United Kingdom than in many others, including countries as varied as Greece, Russia, and Spain. This broken educational system not only stifles social mobility but also depresses labor productivity. To fix it, the government needs to find ways to recruit the best teachers and invest more in training them. At the same time, policymakers should make sure they are using the right yardstick when measuring success. Past attempts at educational reform have failed to improve social mobility, so the government should judge new proposals by how much they will improve the performance of children from disadvantaged backgrounds and not just based on average attainment. The silver lining of the referendum result is that, by highlighting the many places where social mobility is lowest, it appears to have created the political will for such policies.

Public investment in health care would also spur economic activity. Such moves have worked before: government regulation of prices in the NHS forced drug firms to innovate and encouraged competition from low-cost producers; support for biomedical research in public universities in the postwar era helped build a world-class pharmaceutical industry in the United Kingdom. Stepping up health-care spending would not only improve public health but also generate jobs in industries linked to health care and improve corporate bottom lines by creating a healthier work force.

The United Kingdom's problems aren't limited to education and health care, however; the country also spends less on infrastructure than most other rich nations. Many of its roads, houses, and power grids were built in the 1960s and 1970s and are now coming to the ends of their useful lives. The electrical system has deteriorated to the point that earlier this year, the country's energy regulator warned that power shortages could be coming. Investing in infrastructure now would create jobs and lay the foundations for future growth, just as it did for the United States during the Great Depression, when such spending put millions of Americans to work improving the roads and laying the sewer pipes and other equipment that enabled the country's subsequent recovery.

Finally, the British government should ramp up its investments in innovation, focusing on firms that have high growth potential. Innovation produces social benefits—technological advances that can be used in other sectors, for example—beyond the returns to private investors, so it deserves government support. Yet the British government spends much less on promoting innovation than do the governments of France, Germany, and the United States. Since such spending makes workers more efficient, it's no surprise that labor productivity in the United Kingdom is seven to 39 percent lower than it is in those countries.

The British government also does too little to encourage investment in small and medium-sized enterprises, diverting private investments away from young businesses and toward safer activities such as real estate. Smaller companies form the backbone of the British economy, providing 60 percent of private-sector jobs and generating high returns relative to the support they receive. Yet private commercial investors tend to think in the short term and are reluctant to support such businesses, especially during recessions. It wasn't until 2012 that the government attempted to help by setting up the British Business Bank to lend to these firms. And even now, the bank's total lending remains small compared with that of similar facilities in the United States. The government should dramatically scale up the bank's operations.

None of these ideas are radical. But for them to work, politicians must be willing to spend dramatically more than in the past; a few percent of national income will not do the trick.

The Brexit vote has handed the country a gargantuan challenge, and no response to it will satisfy everyone. But if the British government can maintain access to the single market and invest in education, public health, infrastructure, and innovation, then it will contain the immediate damage and may even begin restoring prosperity and hope in the country's forgotten places.

SWATI DHINGRA is Assistant Professor of Economics at the London School of Economics. Follow her on Twitter @swatdhingraLSE.

Pulling the Trigger on Brexit

And Passing the Point of No Return

Matthias Matthijs

European Council President Donald Tusk shows British Prime Minister Theresa May's Brexit letter, Brussels, Belgium, March 29, 2017.

Today, the two-year Brexit clock began its countdown. Now that the British government has formally notified the European Council of its intention to leave the European Union, the United Kingdom has passed the point of no return. It could well turn out to be the biggest act of self-sabotage in modern political history.

Despite what British Foreign Secretary Boris Johnson has promised, the United Kingdom will not be able to have its cake and eat it, too. The rest of the EU is determined to show that leaving the club has negative consequences. And in that sense, by triggering Article 50 of the Lisbon Treaty, the United Kingdom has chosen to relinquish significant control over its own economic future. New trade deals are uncertain and the centrifugal forces of renewed jingoism are beginning to challenge the historic union between England, Wales, Scotland, and Northern Ireland. As a result, the United Kingdom is bound to lose influence on the world stage.

And so, rather than "taking back control," as Brexit supporters have argued, the United Kingdom will lose some autonomy in economic and financial affairs. After all, the biggest barriers to a truly "global Britain" are not trade tariffs but non-tariff regulatory barriers, which require either harmonization across trade partners or, at the very least, mutual recognition. From that point of view, the EU single market was the most ambitious free market experiment in economic history. By leaving it, the United Kingdom is giving up its seat at the European table and will therefore no longer be able to influence future decision-making in its largest market, let alone shape future global regulatory standards. And, by turning its back on the EU Customs Union, it is bound to introduce new barriers to trade.

The United Kingdom in a few years may well exist as the "former United Kingdom of England and Wales," with the unfortunate acronym of FUKEW.

By leaving the EU, meanwhile, the United Kingdom will also lose influence over European foreign policy and thereby see its global clout wane further. Its so-called special relationship with the United States was sustained only by the illusion that the country served as a bridge between Washington and the rest of Europe. Now, even that illusion has been shattered.

The Brexiteers' dream of the United Kingdom reclaiming its rightful place as leader of the Commonwealth or the English-speaking nations—what officials of the country's new Department of International Trade call, without any trace of irony, "Empire 2.0"—is delusional for the simple reason that there is absolutely no demand for it. The United Kingdom will continue to try to punch above its weight in international affairs through an outsize role in NATO, but open hostility of U.S. President Donald Trump and his administration toward the Atlantic alliance makes even that a rather precarious proposition.

Finally, by opting for a "hard" Brexit—meaning leaving both the EU Customs Union and the single market—against the explicit wishes of the people of Scotland and Northern Ireland, British voters have put a dark cloud over the immediate future of the United Kingdom itself. Scottish independence is now more likely than in 2014, and the possible return of a hard border between Northern Ireland and the Republic of Ireland has made the dream of a united Ireland—as envisioned by the Irish republican party Sinn Fein—less far-fetched than it once seemed. The United Kingdom in a few years may well exist as the "former United Kingdom of England and Wales," with the unfortunate acronym of FUKEW.

A few years ago, David Cameron expressed his hope that he would go down as the British prime minister who would have settled his country's two major existential questions: that of EU membership and that of Scotland's future in the United Kingdom. It is fair to say that he has fallen short of his own objective. Now Prime Minister Theresa May has an even more difficult task before her—healing a divided nation while seeking to steer the country out of the EU unscathed. The idea that she will succeed where Cameron failed seems naïve at best.

MATTHIAS MATTHIJS is Assistant Professor in International Political Economy at Johns Hopkins University's School of Advanced International Studies

Theresa May's Gamble

Why Britain's Snap Election Will Do Little to Ease Brexit

Andrew Gawthorpe

Britain's Prime Minister Theresa May attends a campaign event in York, May 9, 2017.

Since her sudden and unexpected call last month for a general election in June, British Prime Minister Theresa May has managed to shed the reputation for indecisiveness that has dogged her since she took power from David Cameron last fall. Also contributing to public perceptions of her strength, she has gone on the attack against the European Union, handily manufacturing a spat by accusing Brussels of seeking to tip the election against her by leaking details of a tense conversation she had recently had with European Commission President Jean-Claude Juncker at a private dinner. As can be expected, the admixture of nationalist posturing to political combat has proven intoxicating. The woman once nicknamed "Theresa Maybe" has now been recast by the press as the reincarnation of Boudicca, a warrior queen who led ancient Britons in a revolt against Roman occupation.

All signs point to a dramatic victory for May's Conservative Party in the upcoming election, scheduled to take place on June 8. Many observers hope that an increased parliamentary majority will free May from the right wing of her own party, which is pushing for the United Kingdom to drive what many consider an unrealistically hard bargain in its negotiations with Brussels. With such voices sidelined, she would be able to make compromises with the EU that will mitigate the damage of its departure. Apparently anticipating just such a result, money markets have grown more optimistic about the United Kingdom since the election was announced.

But such an outcome is far from assured. In particular, the British government needs to be careful not to let its campaign rhetoric—such as accusing the "bureaucrats of Brussels" of using "threats" to interfere with Britain's democratic process—damage its chances of securing a productive arrangement with the EU over the long term. Brexit is an idea that has always sounded better when discussed in the abstract rather than in detail, but eventually London will have to move from rhetoric to reality.

POLITICAL SHIFT

The surge in support for the Conservative Party and the collapse of its rivals, the center–left Labour and the far–right United Kingdom Independence Party, is stunning. Opinion polls currently give the Conservatives a 20-point lead over Labour, while support for UKIP has atrophied since the Conservatives became the standard-bearers for its signature issue—leaving the EU. The Labour Party is floundering under its far–left leader Jeremy Corbyn, who also backs Brexit but is unpopular among the ageing, provincial voters who form the backbone of support for exiting the EU.

Recent local election results, in which the Conservatives enjoyed their best performance in a decade, suggest that the Conservatives could be on their way to a working parliamentary majority of over 100, a dramatic improvement on their current 17. May has claimed that she is seeking a large majority to show Brussels how united the British people are behind her Brexit strategy. In reality, the British are more divided over Brexit than ever, with a poll recently showing for the first time that a plurality of voters regret the decision to leave the EU. But with Labour attempting to make up the ground it had lost to UKIP over the last decade by backing Brexit, only smaller parties with no chance of forming a government are campaigning on the basis of staying in the EU. As a result, Europhile voters are short of options and May faces no credible threats on the political horizon.

This does not mean that she will find it any easier to demand concessions from Brussels after the election. The EU, which thinks in terms of international and intragovernmental obligations, has no reason to back down simply because its negotiating partner has strong domestic support. In fact, policymakers in Brussels and

Berlin actually want May to succeed for the opposite reason: a larger parliamentary bloc will also give her more room to make concessions. That is why May's accusations that Brussels is trying to undermine her position in the upcoming election makes so little sense: no one on the continent benefits from her remaining in thrall to the unrealistic demands of her own party's right wing.

MUGGED BY REALITY

The Conservative right remains the largest threat to an eventual agreement between the EU and the United Kingdom. Egged on by a belligerent nationalist press, many Conservative lawmakers claim that it would be better for the United Kingdom to crash out of the EU without reaching any agreement on a future relationship. This would allow London to avoid concessions on issues such as paying unmet financial obligations, immigration, and the continued jurisdiction of European courts in the United Kingdom. But it would also mean that the United Kingdom would lose privileged access to the market to which it currently sends 44 percent of its exports. The understaffed British civil service has not yet fully worked out what the consequences of such a move would be, but it looks likely to amount to around $7.2 billion in tariffs for British exporters per year.

The right's tough stance is based on the false promises of the Leave campaign, which promoted the idea that the United Kingdom could cut immigration from the EU while maintaining access to the common market. Many Leave campaigners incorrectly portrayed the EU as being on the brink of collapse and therefore desperate to make concessions to the United Kingdom. They also suggested that London would be able to cut separate bilateral deals with countries such as Germany in the aftermath of Brexit. But with the eurozone economy growing faster than both the United Kingdom's and the United States', the issue of migration crisis having waned, and anti-EU political forces pushed back in Austria, France, Germany, and the Netherlands, cracks in the bloc are no longer so obvious. At a recent summit meeting, it took less than 15 minutes for the member states to agree on their common negotiating stance toward the British. The EU's position includes several points anathema to the United Kingdom, including having London settle its financial obligations and reach an agreement on the rights of EU citizens currently in the country before any discussion of their future relationship can proceed.

As Brussels fails to bend, British right–wing politicians and tabloids have responded by blaming the EU for what they see as intransigence and by suggesting that the prime minister must "crush the saboteurs" who they say want to undermine an agreement. By threatening to walk away from the talks and directing her fire at domestic opponents, May is now flirting with these political passions, even if she hopes to eventually sideline them. But the other 27 EU member states have domestic politics too. Following the election of France's Emmanuel Macron and the likely reelection of German Chancellor Angela Merkel in September, both Paris and Berlin will be absorbed by their own priorities to push through economic reform in pursuit of eurozone stability and growth. They are bound by their own national interests, as well as those of the bloc as a whole, to take a tough stance against a country that has chosen to make itself increasingly irrelevant to their future concerns.

There is also a risk that the increasingly poisonous tone of British political discourse will harden the hearts of other European electorates, and hence their governments, toward the United Kingdom. The German government, as the paymaster of Europe, is under severe domestic pressure not to let the United Kingdom dilute the Brexit financial settlement in the way British politicians argue they can. Meanwhile Poland, which under different circumstances might be one of the main proponents of an amicable Brexit, has first and foremost to protect the interests of the large Polish diaspora in the United Kingdom. This British sojourn into hardline campaigning for the snap election means serious discussions on such issues cannot begin until June, wasting two months of the brief two-year period that London has to reach an agreement with the EU on their future relationship.

If May's gamble pays off, she will be able to tame her party's right wing, reach a favorable and moderate agreement with the EU, and go into the next election in 2022 as the prime minister who delivered a successful Brexit. But she risks losing it all if she continues to pose as Boudicca when Brussels refuses to follow the script that British nationalists want it to. The stakes for both the prime minister and the country are high. Both May and the country at large will soon have to stop electioneering, honestly assess the cards they hold, and start dealing.

ANDREW GAWTHORPE is a Lecturer in History and International Studies at Leiden University in The Netherlands. He formerly worked in the British Cabinet Office.

© Foreign Affairs

France's Next Revolution?

A Conversation With Marine Le Pen

HEINZ-PETER BADER / REUTERS

Le Pen in Vienna, June 2016.

As the youngest daughter of Jean-Marie Le Pen, the founder of the right-wing French political party the National Front, Marine Le Pen grew up in politics, starting to campaign with her father at 13. Trained as a lawyer, she won her first election in 1998, as a regional councilor, and in 2011, she succeeded her father as party leader. She soon distanced herself from his more extreme positions, and eventually—after he reiterated his claim that the Holocaust was a "detail" of history—she expelled him from its ranks. These days, in the wake of the European migrant crisis, the terrorist attacks in Paris and Nice, and the Brexit vote, Le Pen's nationalist, Euroskeptical, anti-immigrant message is selling well. Recent polls show her as a leading candidate for the presidency in 2017, with respondents preferring her two to one over the Socialist incumbent, François Hollande. Le Pen spoke with Foreign Affairs' deputy managing editor Stuart Reid in Paris in September.

Lire en français (Read in French).

ANTIESTABLISHMENT PARTIES, INCLUDING THE NATIONAL FRONT, ARE GAINING GROUND ACROSS EUROPE. HOW COME?

I believe that all people aspire to be free. For too long, the people of the countries in the European Union, and perhaps Americans as well, have had a sense that political leaders are not defending their interests but defending special interests instead. There is a form of revolt on the part of the people against a system that is no longer serving them but rather serving itself.

ARE THERE COMMON FACTORS BEHIND DONALD TRUMP'S SUCCESS IN THE UNITED STATES AND YOURS HERE IN FRANCE?

Yes. I see particular commonalities in the rise of Donald Trump and Bernie Sanders. Both reject a system that appears to be very selfish, even egocentric, and that has set aside the people's aspirations. I draw a parallel between the two, because they are both success stories. Even though Bernie Sanders didn't win, his emergence wasn't predicted. In many countries, there is this current of being attached to the nation and rejecting untamed globalization, which is seen as a form of totalitarianism. It's being imposed at all costs, a war against everybody for the benefit of a few.

WHEN ASKED RECENTLY WHO YOU SUPPORTED IN THE U.S. ELECTION, YOU SAID, "ANYONE BUT HILLARY." SO DO YOU SUPPORT TRUMP?

I was quite clear: in my view, anyone would be better than Hillary Clinton. I aim to become president of the French Republic, so I am concerned exclusively with the interests of France. I cannot put myself in an American's shoes and determine whether the domestic policies proposed by one or another candidate suit me. What interests me are the consequences of the political choices made by Hillary Clinton or Donald Trump for France's situation, economically and in terms of security.

So I would note that Clinton supports TTIP [the Transatlantic Trade and Investment Partnership]. Trump opposes it. I oppose it as well. I would also note that Clinton is a bringer of war in the world, leaving behind her Iraq, Libya, and Syria. This has had extremely destabilizing consequences for my country in terms of the rise of Islamic fundamentalism and the enormous waves of migration now overwhelming the European Union. Trump wants the United States to return to its natural state. Clinton pushes for the extraterritorial application of American law, which is an unacceptable weapon for people who wish to remain independent. All of this tells me that between Hillary Clinton and Donald Trump, it's Donald Trump's policies that are more favorable to France's interests right now.

Aboard the aircraft carrier Charles de Gaulle, Toulon, France, November 2015.

THE UNEMPLOYMENT RATE IN FRANCE NOW STANDS AT AROUND TEN PERCENT, THE SECOND HIGHEST AMONG THE G-7 MEMBERS. WHAT ARE THE ROOTS OF FRANCE'S ECONOMIC MALAISE, AND WHAT SOLUTIONS DO YOU PROPOSE?

These days, everyone is proposing the National Front's solutions. We recorded a nice ideological victory when I heard [Arnaud] Montebourg [a former economy minister in Hollande's Socialist government] pleading for "made in France," which is one of the major pillars of the National Front.

The unemployment rate is much higher than that because there are a bunch of statistical shenanigans going on—involving internships, early retirement, part-time work—that keep a number of French from being counted in the unemployment statistics.

There are a number of reasons for [the high unemployment]. The first is completely free trade, which puts us in an unfair competition with countries that engage in social and environmental dumping, leaving us with no means of protecting ourselves and our strategic companies, unlike in the United States. And in terms of social dumping, the Posted Workers Directive [an EU directive on the free movement of labor] is bringing low-wage employees to France.

The second is the monetary dumping we suffer. The euro—the fact of not having our own money—puts us in an extremely difficult economic situation. The IMF has just said that the euro was overvalued by six percent in France and undervalued by 15 percent in Germany. That's a gap of 21 percentage points with our main competitor in Europe.

It also has to do with the disappearance of a strategic state. Our very Gaullist state, which supported our industrial champions, has been totally abandoned. France is a country of engineers. It is a country of researchers. But it's true that it is not a country of businesspeople. And so quite often in history, our big industrial champions were able to develop only thanks to the strategic state. In abandoning this, we are depriving ourselves of a very important lever for development.

LET'S TALK ABOUT ABANDONING THE EURO. PRACTICALLY SPEAKING, HOW WOULD YOU DO IT?

What I want is a negotiation. What I want is a concerted exit from the European Union, where all the countries sit around the table and decide to return to the European "currency snake" [a 1970s policy designed to limit exchange-rate variations], which allows each country to adapt its monetary policy to its own economy. That's what I want. I want it to be done gently and in a coordinated manner.

A lot of countries are now realizing that they can't keep living with the euro, because its counterpart is a policy of austerity, which has aggravated the recession in various countries. I refer you to the book that [the economist Joseph] Stiglitz has just written, which makes very clear that this currency is completely maladapted to our economies and is one of the reasons there is so much unemployment in the European Union. So either we get there through negotiation, or we hold a referendum like Britain and decide to regain control of our currency.

DO YOU REALLY THINK A "FREXIT" REFERENDUM IS CONCEIVABLE?

I, at any rate, am conceiving of it. The French people were betrayed in 2005. They said no to the European constitution; politicians on the right and the left imposed it against the wishes of the population. I'm a democrat. I think that it is up to no one else but the French people to decide their future and everything that affects their sovereignty, liberty, and independence.

So yes, I would organize a referendum on this subject. And based on what happened in the negotiations that I would undertake, I would tell the French, "Listen, I obtained what I wanted, and I think we could stay in the European Union," or, "I did not get what I wanted, and I believe there is no other solution but to leave the European Union."

WHAT LESSONS DO YOU TAKE FROM THE SUCCESS OF THE BREXIT CAMPAIGN?

Two major lessons. First, when the people want something, nothing is impossible. And second, we were lied to. They told us that Brexit would be a catastrophe, that the stock markets would crash, that the economy was going to grind to a halt, that unemployment would skyrocket. The reality is that none of that happened. Today, the banks are coming to us pitifully and saying, "Ah, we were wrong." No, you lied to us. You lied in order to influence the vote. But the people are coming to know your methods, which consist of terrorizing them when they have a choice to make. The British people made a great show of maturity with this vote.

DO YOU WORRY THAT FRANCE WILL FIND ITSELF ECONOMICALLY ISOLATED IF IT LEAVES THE EUROZONE?

Those were the exact criticisms made against General de Gaulle in 1966 when he wanted to withdraw from NATO's integrated command. Freedom is not isolation. Independence is not isolation. And what strikes me is that France has always been much more powerful being France on its own than being a province of the European Union. I want to rediscover that strength.

MANY CREDIT THE EUROPEAN UNION FOR PRESERVING THE PEACE SINCE WORLD WAR II. WHY ARE THEY WRONG?

Because it's not the European Union that has kept the peace; it's the peace that has made the European Union possible. This argument has been rehashed repeatedly, and it makes no sense. Regardless, the peace hasn't been perfect in the European Union, with Kosovo and Ukraine at its doorstep. It's not so simple.

In fact, the European Union has progressively transformed itself into a sort of European Soviet Union that decides everything, that imposes its views, that shuts down the democratic process. You only have to hear [European Commission President Jean-Claude] Juncker, who said, "There can be no democratic choice against European treaties." That formulation says everything. We didn't fight to become a free and independent people during World War I and World War II so that we could no longer be free today just because some of our leaders made that decision for us.

German Chancellor Angela Merkel and French President Francois Hollande in Evian, France, September 2016.

WHAT DO YOU MAKE OF GERMANY'S LEADERSHIP IN RECENT YEARS?

It was written into the creation of the euro. In reality, the euro is a currency created by Germany, for Germany. It's a suit that fits only Germany. Gradually, [Chancellor Angela] Merkel sensed that she was the leader of the European Union. She imposed her views. She imposed them in economic matters, but she also imposed them by agreeing to welcome one million migrants to Germany, knowing very well that Germany would sort them out. It would keep the best and let the rest go to other countries in the European Union. There are no longer any internal borders between our countries, which is absolutely unacceptable. The model imposed by Merkel surely works for Germans, but it is killing Germany's neighbors. I am the anti-Merkel.

WHAT DO YOU THINK OF THE STATE OF RELATIONS BETWEEN FRANCE AND THE UNITED STATES, AND WHAT SHOULD THEY BE?

Today, French leaders submit so easily to the demands of Merkel and Obama. France has forgotten to defend its interests, including its commercial and industrial ones, in the face of American demands. I am for independence. I am for a France that remains equidistant between the two great powers, Russia and the United States, being neither submissive nor hostile. I want us to once again become a leader for the nonaligned countries, as was said during the de Gaulle era. We have the right to defend our interests, just as the United States has the right to defend its interests, Germany has the right to defend its interests, and Russia has the right to defend its interests.

WHY DO YOU THINK FRANCE SHOULD GET CLOSER TO RUSSIA UNDER PRESIDENT VLADIMIR PUTIN?

First of all, because Russia is a European country. France and Russia also have a shared history and a strong cultural affinity. And strategically, there is no reason not to deepen relations with Russia. The only reason we don't is because the Americans forbid it. That conflicts with my desire for independence. What's more, I think the United States is making a mistake by re-creating a kind of cold war with Russia, because it's pushing Russia into the arms of China. And objectively, an ultrapowerful association between China and Russia wouldn't be advantageous for either the United States or the world.

IN THE LATEST POLLS, THE NATIONAL FRONT IS PROJECTED TO MAKE IT TO THE RUNOFF OF THE PRESIDENTIAL ELECTION. IN THE PAST, NOTABLY IN 2002, THE OTHER PARTIES UNITED TO BLOCK THE NATIONAL FRONT IN THE SECOND ROUND. WOULD YOU BE READY TO FORM ALLIANCES, AND IF SO, WITH WHOM?

It's not up to me to decide that. This presidential election will be about a big choice: Do we defend our civilization, or do we abandon it? So I think there are people from the entire political spectrum, from the right and the left, who agree with me and who could join us.

THE NATIONAL FRONT THAT YOU ARE LEADING HAS CHANGED A GREAT DEAL FROM THE PARTY YOUR FATHER LED. AT WHAT POINT IN YOUR CAREER DID YOU REALIZE THAT THE NATIONAL FRONT HAD TO DISTANCE ITSELF FROM ITS EXTREMIST IMAGE IF IT WAS GOING TO BE COMPETITIVE?

In the past, the National Front was a protest party. It was an opposition party. Naturally, its rising influence has transformed it into a party of government—that is, into a party that anticipates reaching the highest offices in order to implement its ideas. It's also true that a political movement is always influenced by its leader's personality. I have not taken the same path as my father. I am not the same age as he is. I do not have the same profile. He is a man; I am a woman. And that means I have imprinted on the party an image that corresponds more with who I am than with who he was.

YOUSSEF BOUDLAL / REUTERS

At a mosque in Paris, January 2015.

HOW CAN FRANCE PROTECT ITSELF FROM TERRORIST ATTACKS LIKE THE ONE IN NICE IN JULY?

So far, it has done absolutely nothing. It has to stop the arrival of migrants, whom we know terrorists infiltrate. It has to put an end to birthright citizenship, the automatic acquisition of French nationality with no other criteria that created French like [Amedy] Coulibaly and [Chérif and Saïd] Kouachi [the terrorists behind the Paris attacks of January 2015], who had long histories of delinquency and were hostile toward France. This isn't the case for everyone; I'm not generalizing. But it's a good way to have a surveillance mechanism. We need to revoke citizenship from dual nationals who have any kind of link to terrorist organizations.

We especially need to combat the development of Islamic fundamentalism on our territory. For electoral reasons, French politicians rolled out the red carpet for Islamic fundamentalism, which has developed in mosques and so-called cultural centers financed not only by France but also by countries that support Islamic fundamentalism. We also have to regain the mastery of our borders, because I can't see how we can combat terrorism while having open borders.

YOU HAVE SAID THAT APART FROM ISLAM, "NO OTHER RELIGION CAUSES PROBLEMS." WHY DO YOU THINK THAT THIS IS TRUE?

Because all religions in France are subject to the rules of secularism. Let's be clear, many Muslims have done that. But some within Islam—and of course I'm thinking of the Islamic fundamentalists—cannot accept that, for one simple reason, which is that they consider sharia to be superior to all other laws and norms, including the French constitution. That's unacceptable.

For a century, since the law on secularism was passed, no one has sought to impose religious law by bending the laws of our country. These Islamic fundamentalist groups are seeking to do this. This must be said, because we cannot fight an enemy if we do not name it. We must be intransigent when it comes to respecting our constitution and our laws. And honestly, the French political class has instead acted in the spirit of Canadian-style reasonable accommodation rather than in the spirit of an intransigence that would allow us to protect our civil liberties. We see it in the huge regressions in women's rights taking place today on French soil. In certain areas, women can no longer dress as they wish.

YOU SUPPORT THE BAN ON THE BURKINI. WHY IS IT A PROBLEM?

The problem is that it's not a bathing suit. It's an Islamist uniform. It's one of the many ways in which Islamic fundamentalism flexes its muscles. Once we accept that women are subject to this Islamist uniform, the next step is that we accept the separation of the sexes in swimming pools and other public spaces. And then we'll have to accept different rights for men and women. If you don't see that, then you don't understand the battle we face against Islamic fundamentalism.

BUT DOES THIS MEASURE REALLY HELP INTEGRATE MUSLIMS IN FRANCE?

What is integration? It is to live side by side, each with their own lifestyle, their own code, their own mores, their own language. The French model is assimilation. Individual freedom does not allow one to call into question the major civilizational choices France has made.

In France, we don't believe in the concept of a consenting victim. French criminal law, for example, doesn't allow people to harm themselves on the grounds that they have the right to do so because they are acting on their own. We don't accept that, because it undermines the major choices we have made as a civilization regarding women's equality and the rejection of communitarianism—that is, organized communities that live according to their own rules. That is the Anglo-Saxon model. It is not ours. The Anglo-Saxons have the right to defend their model, but we have the right to defend ours.

DO YOU THINK THAT THE AMERICAN MODEL OF INTEGRATION IS MORE EFFECTIVE THAN THE FRENCH ONE?

I don't have to judge that. That's a problem for Americans. Personally, I don't want that model. That model is a consequence of American history. Communities came from different countries to a virgin land to create a nation made up of people from everywhere. That is not the case for France. France is a very old human and legal creation. Nothing is there by chance. Secularism is how we handled religious conflicts that had plunged our country into a bloodbath.

I don't seek to impose my model on others, but I don't want others to decide that my model is not the right one. I'm often offended when foreign countries condemn the French model.

I don't condemn the American model. But I don't want mine condemned. I think that communitarianism sows the seeds of conflict between communities, and I don't want my country to face conflicts between communities. I recognize only individuals. It is individuals who have rights. It is individuals who have free will. It is individuals who assimilate themselves. In no case is it communities.

This interview has been translated from the French, edited, and condensed.

Europe in Russia's Digital Cross Hairs

What's Next for France and Germany—and How to Deal With It

Thorsten Benner and Mirko Hohmann

German Chancellor Angela Merkel, Russian President Vladimir Putin, and French President Francois Hollande at the Kremlin, February 2015.

In recent weeks, politicians and intelligence officials in France and Germany have stepped up their warnings of Russian interference in the national elections both countries will hold next year. In late November, Bruno Kahl, the head of Germany's Federal Intelligence Service, told the Süddeutsche Zeitung that Germany had "evidence that cyberattacks are taking place that have no purpose other than to elicit political uncertainty." German Chancellor Angela Merkel has expressed similar concerns, suggesting that Moscow may attempt to influence Germany's parliamentary elections, which are slated for September 2017. French politicians have been more circumspect about the specific threats posed to their country's presidential elections, which will be held in April and May. But Guillaume Poupard, the director-general of France's National Agency for the Security of Information Systems, has indicated that Paris, too, is concerned about the prospect of foreign interference. Western democracies face "the development of a digital threat for political ends and for destabilization," he told Le Monde in early December.

Neither France nor Germany, however, is ready to deal with such attacks. Their institutions are ill-equipped to prevent digital breaches, and their politicians and publics are unprepared to handle the fallout from them.

To better understand the threat they face, leaders in both countries would do well to learn from the most brazen Russian-led influence operation so far: the leaking of information stolen from servers of the Democratic National Committee (DNC) and the private email account of John Podesta, the chairman of Hillary Clinton's presidential campaign. A careful look at that episode and its aftermath demonstrates the importance of strengthening the cyberdefenses of democratic institutions, building a political consensus to condemn attacks, and publicly naming—and punishing—the perpetrators.

Stefanie Loos / REUTERS

Visitors tour the grounds of the German Federal Intelligence Service in Berlin, August 2016.

COMPROMISED

The use of incriminating information to publicly discredit opponents is widespread, but Russian intelligence services have a particularly strong penchant for the tactic. During the Cold War, the practice was common enough that the Russian term kompromat (a portmanteau combining the Russian words for "compromising" and "material") entered the Western vernacular.

Today's digital communications offer those seeking to gather and exploit kompromat enormous advantages relative to their Cold War–era counterparts. It is now easier than it was during the twentieth century to quickly obtain vast amounts of sensitive information, in part because the digital networks of key institutions are difficult to secure. Completely safeguarding a platform used by hundreds or thousands of people, such as that of a political party, is nearly impossible. And once attackers access sensitive information, they can easily release it, sometimes in altered form, to the public. Consider the speed at which the DNC's and Podesta's hacked emails moved from WikiLeaks and social media to state-sponsored news outlets such as RT, far-right sites such as Breitbart, and mainstream news organizations. All these factors make the work of hackers hard to counter, let alone contain.

Kompromat operations do not always seek to promote particular candidates, even though Russia's interventions in the U.S. election clearly meant to elevate Donald Trump. (French officials should expect similar moves in support of National Front leader Marine Le Pen in the coming months.) The goal is usually broader: to corrode democratic norms and institutions by discrediting the electoral process and to tarnish the reputations of democratic governments in order to establish a kind of moral equivalence between Russia and the West. From the Kremlin's perspective, attacks on democratic political institutions are a form of payback for what it perceives as the West's longstanding attempts to hem in and undermine Russia—most recently, the leak of the Panama Papers, which pointed to the cronyism of Russian President Vladimir Putin's inner circle and which Russian authorities attributed to Washington, and the anti-government demonstrations that roiled Russian cities after the country's election in 2011. Putin accused Hillary Clinton, then the U.S. secretary of state, of instigating those protests.

TOO LITTLE, TOO LATE

As Thomas Rid, a leading analyst of intelligence operations, has noted, Russia's attempt to undermine the U.S. election was "innovative, bold, shrewd, cost-effective, professional (largely), [and] very hard to counter." Yet the degree to which U.S. institutions were blindsided by the attack remains astonishing.

Given Clinton's own experience with controversies related to email security, her campaign's digital communications should have been ironclad. Instead, one of the

Clinton campaign's own network administrators cleared as legitimate—apparently as a result of a typo—a spearphishing attack that may have let Russian hackers into Podesta's account. The DNC apparently neither used state-of-the-art security software, nor did it have a budget large enough to hire the professional staff required to protect its networks. DNC officials did not even respond to the messages that intelligence officials left on their answering machines weeks after the first warnings of a potential attack.

French and German officials should assume that hackers have tapped the systems of political parties and have sifted through the emails of potential candidates.

Even more surprising was the U.S. government's apparent lack of preparation for such a contingency. Once the administration of President Barack Obama became aware of the extent of the attack, it scrambled to develop a coherent response. The FBI was apparently aware of the initial intrusions into the DNC's systems in late 2015, and the security firm Crowdstrike published a report linking the hack to the Russian government in June 2016. But even then, it took the Obama administration until October to do the same, and it changed tack only under intense pressure from Congress. To make matters worse, the administration announced Russia's involvement on a Friday evening, as the public's attention was consumed by Hurricane Matthew, and it failed to publicly outline any measures it would take to punish the attackers or their sponsors.

The administration's reluctance may have stemmed from an understandable fear of appearing partisan, but in light of the serious challenges to U.S. security posed by Russia's actions, it was the wrong call. The White House should have publicly implicated Russia soon after the evidence was available in the summer. It should have outlined clear political consequences for Moscow. And, along with the DNC, it should have done more to establish a bipartisan consensus around condemning Russia's actions—before November 8.

THE DNC'S LESSONS

As their own elections approach, French and German policymakers should learn from the United States' recent experience. There are a number of steps Berlin and Paris can take to protect their institutions and discourage Russia from carrying out the same kinds of actions in Europe as it has in the United States.

Both countries should harden the cyberdefenses of key democratic institutions, such as political parties, federal and state-level parliaments, and government agencies. These organizations form the backbones of democratic societies and should receive the highest level of state protection; at the moment, that is not generally the case. The EU has already defined parliaments and government institutions as critical infrastructures, or systems that are "essential for the maintenance of vital societal functions," and European governments should deliver on their promises to protect them. Information-security agencies, such as Germany's Federal Office for Information Security, should assume a deeper role in helping political parties prevent and react to attacks. More broadly, states should take breaches of political institutions as seriously as they would violations of telecommunications networks or power grids, if not more so.

Next, European countries should classify the electoral processes by which ballots are cast and counted as critical infrastructure, thus qualifying them, too, for a higher degree of government protection. States should ban the use of electronic voting machines, using paper ballots instead. In its conversations with China and Russia on cybersecurity norms, Europe should make clear that electoral processes (including voter registries) should be off-limits from cyberattacks and signal that future interference in them would lead to serious consequences.

Both France and Germany should incentivize political parties to improve their digital security. Parties' fears of public leaks has probably already made them more cautious, but Berlin and Paris should also offer the services of state information agencies to interested parties and their top staff members. If certain parties, especially from the opposition, are not willing to let officials access their servers, the government should offer to pay for them to hire private security companies. France and Germany should also work with allies and private firms to improve their ability to trace the origins of attacks.

A police officer stands guard in front of the offices of TV5Monde, a French television outlet targeted in a cyberattack, Paris, April 2015.

MAKING MOSCOW PAY

Such precautions could help safeguard elections in the future, yet they may do little to protect next year's votes. Russian-backed hackers successfully infiltrated the German parliament's servers a year ago. French and German officials should assume that hackers have also tapped the systems of political parties and have sifted through the emails of potential candidates and their associates.

That makes preparing for the political consequences of future leaks even more important. In Germany, Merkel has rightly spoken about potential electoral interference, helping ready Germans for the shock of future leaks. French political leaders should follow suit. Given that Russian involvement in France's electoral politics is already well-established, French officials may be tempted to overlook the new threats posed by digital kompromat. But that would be a mistake, especially since it will be harder for parties to stand together against such actions, regardless of whom they affect, once their campaigns are under way.

In both France and Germany, parties should publicly promise not to use leaked information for political gain. Parties in other European countries should join them:

a united European effort would serve as a stronger deterrent. If some parties, such as the National Front or Germany's Alternative for Germany, choose not to commit to such a pact, other parties should commit themselves anyway, and they should raise the refusal of their counterparts to do the same in public debates.

That will not be enough, however, since stolen information will spread in the media regardless of how parties handle it. Boycotting reporting on leaked information is not a reasonable option, since doing so would leave coverage to fringe outlets and would constitute a troubling form of self-censorship. But publishers should regard the information provided by enablers such as WikiLeaks more critically, working to establish, for example, which leaked documents have been tampered with. More broadly, media outlets should develop codes of conduct that clarify how they should handle massive tranches of leaked information.

Merkel has spoken about potential electoral interference, helping ready Germans for the shock of future leaks.

Finally, France and Germany need to show that there will be consequences for foreign nations that interfere in their electoral processes. European governments could expel Russian diplomats, for example, or discuss imposing EU sanctions on Russia or Russian officials, depending on the scale of the interference. France and Germany should try to persuade NATO members to designate the most severe attacks on electoral processes as sufficient to trigger the alliance's mutual-defense guarantee, and they should outline how NATO would respond to such attacks up front. NATO's countermeasures should focus on demonstrating the alliance's offensive cyber capacities to Russia—for example, by taking the networks of hackers involved in past attacks offline. Imposing such costs would help to deter future meddling. And although doing so would risk provoking further retaliation, it would be better than not reacting, which would leave the initiative for escalation entirely in Russia's hands.

Europe, however, should not respond to political-influence operations in kind. The information gathered by Western intelligence agencies should be used for decision-making and to inform private communications with Russian officials, but the West should not leak it in an attempt to undermine the Russian government. That would only serve to legitimize the tactic.

So far, Russia has managed to carry out such operations at little political cost. Moscow will continue doing so in the run-up to the French and German elections, and given how unprepared both countries are for that possibility, it will probably succeed. The Netherlands, which will hold elections in March, is another possible target, as is Italy, which may hold elections next year. Better managing the threat of influence operations and ensuring that attackers pay a price for carrying them out would help preserve the integrity of European democracies and deter similar actions by Russia and other illiberal powers in the future.

THORSTEN BENNER is Co-Founder and Director of the Global Public Policy Institute, in Berlin. Follow him on Twitter @thorstenbenner. MIRKO HOHMANN is a project manager at the Global Public Policy Institute. Follow him on Twitter @mirkohohmann.

Macron's Victory

Why French Voters Rejected Le Pen

Arthur Goldhammer

CHRISTIAN HARTMANN / REUTERS

Emmanuel Macron in Paris, France, April 17, 2017.

Emmanuel Macron, the 39-year-old former economy minister who grew up as the son of two doctors in the provincial backwater of Amiens, will be the next president of France, having won with around 66 percent of the vote. Although he has never held elective office, he defeated the redoubtable Marine Le Pen, the heiress to a populist dynasty founded by her father, Jean-Marie Le Pen, who defended torture in Algeria, called Nazi gas chambers a mere "detail" of history, and once punched a female Socialist politician in the face.

The Le Pens have adopted Joan of Arc as their hero. Joan, a child of the people who is considered by some the "mother of the French nation," heard voices that told her to boot foreigners—the English—out of France. The Le Pens hearken to the same voices, although the identity of the foreigner has changed.

In this election, however, it is Macron who appears to have been listening to otherwise unheard voices. While still serving under outgoing President François Hollande, the fledgling economy minister hatched a plan to replace his boss. After he founded a movement called En Marche! (Onward!) in April 2016, advisers warned Hollande that the man whom the president had once described as his spiritual son was preparing to run against him. Yet despite long years as a political insider, Hollande dismissed such rumors.

The young prodigy's remarkable rise began when he graduated near the top of his class from the highly selective National School of Administration, the nursery of the French elite. This gave him entry into the most prestigious of France's administrative corps, the Inspectorate General of Finance. He thus began his career already near the top of the ladder. After a short detour into the private sector, where he spent a few years working as an investment banker, Macron returned to government as a senior member of Hollande's staff. From there he was appointed economy minister, a post from which he resigned in August 2016 to devote himself full-time to running for president.

Macron's platform combined business-friendly reforms such as labor-market deregulation with promises to invest in green jobs and decrease French dependence on fossil fuels. He favors a Scandinavian-style "flexicurity" model, in which workers are supported while transitioning from jobs in declining sectors to jobs (hopefully) created in rising sectors. Of all the candidates in the race, he was the staunchest defender of the European Union and the most adamant in insisting that French industry must adapt to become more competitive in the globalized economy.

In a period of rebellion against "elites" everywhere, many observers feared that the French would follow the surly majorities that took the United Kingdom out of the European Union and elected Donald Trump as president of the United States. France did not lack for angry voters. Populist insurgencies rose on both the left and right flanks. On the left, Jean-Luc Mélenchon's France Insoumise (France Unbowed) movement attracted more than 19 percent of the first-round vote. In the final two weeks before the vote, Mélenchon rose so rapidly that some feared the final runoff could be a contest between left and right extremes. In the end, however, he fell short. And Le Pen, who inherited leadership of the National Front from her father in 2011, did less well than early polls had predicted, scoring just 21.3 percent, well below her polling peak of 28 percent. Macron led the field with a comfortable 24 percent.

This strong first-round finish set the stage for Macron's success in the runoff. Le Pen read the polls and apparently concluded that although her efforts to "de-demonize" the party by purging it of anti-Semites and neo-Nazis had steadily increased its vote share in successive elections, she could not win the presidency without some bold surprises in the homestretch. Attempting to emulate former President Charles de Gaulle's claim to rise above party, on April 24, one day after the first-round vote, she abruptly resigned from her presidency of the National Front and named the little-known Jean-François Jalkh to replace her. But he turned out to be a Holocaust denier, reminding voters of the unsavory past she had so assiduously sought to lay to rest.

Compounding her error, Le Pen then flip-flopped on her signature issue: a promise to hold an immediate referendum on French withdrawal from the European Union. Like Trump, she had attracted the support of workers (the National Front now receives more working-class votes than any other party) by promising to erect protectionist barriers in order to restore jobs outsourced to low-wage countries. She was lionized in Macron's hometown of Amiens when she appeared at a Whirlpool plant, the imminent closure of which will result in several hundred jobs being shipped to Poland. Her promise of a 35 percent tariff on imports from firms that outsourced jobs proved popular among workers, but it is a promise she cannot fulfill as long as France remains in the EU.

Since polls show that approximately 70 percent of the French are wary of leaving the EU, especially since the Brexit vote and Trump's expressions of hostility toward the EU and NATO, Le Pen apparently concluded that she could not win the presidency without allaying fears of an abrupt Frexit. So she backtracked. Her niece Marion Maréchal-Le Pen announced on April 30 that instead of holding a referendum on exiting the EU within six months of the election, as originally promised, there would be "a lengthy process," lasting perhaps "several years," because the original proposal was neither practical nor legal under existing treaties.

Le Pen also retreated from the second pillar of her economic program: a promise to abandon the euro. She remained opposed to "the single currency," she said, but saw nothing wrong with a "common currency," leaving voters scratching their heads as to what she meant.

The last-minute obfuscations raised doubts about her competence—doubts that were compounded by her bizarre, brutally aggressive performance in the final debate of the campaign. Through much of the multi-hour affair, she wore what many observers called a sinister smile, sneering at and mocking her opponent's challenges to her economic policies and refusing to make the slightest concession to expectations that she might wish to appear "more presidential." It was a ploy borrowed from Trump's playbook: rather than engage with her opponent, she mocked his alleged elitism with a display of petulant vulgarity.

It worked for Trump, but not for Le Pen. Postdebate polls showed a sharp bounce for Macron. The French may not like their elites, but they expect a certain decorum from their presidents. At an agricultural fair in Paris on February 2008, then President Nicolas Sarkozy triggered a backlash when he told a heckler to "buzz off." Le Pen's crude pugnacity recalled her father's verbal (and physical) bullying. In the end she frightened more voters with her radicalism than she attracted with her attempt to cast herself as the stalwart defender of "republican values" and "national identity," which she claimed were under assault from alien elements, especially Muslim immigrants.

The final vote was more a rejection of Le Penism, however, than an affirmation of support for Macron, who now faces the challenge of governing the country without an established party to lend him support in the National Assembly. Legislative elections slated for June will thus determine how strong a hand the new president will have in pushing through the reforms he thinks are necessary but about which many who voted for him remain skeptical.

ARTHUR GOLDHAMMER is an American academic and translator based at the Minda de Gunzburg Center for European Studies at Harvard.

Austria's Populist Puzzle

Why One of Europe's Most Stable States Hosts a Thriving Radical Right

Reinhard Heinisch

A worker passes presidential election campaign posters for Norbert Hofer and Alexander Van der Bellen in Vienna, September 2016.

For many international observers, Austria's flirtation with right-wing populism is something of a puzzle. Austria is one of the European Union's most prosperous countries and has long been a model of political and social stability. It has an efficient government, excellent public infrastructure, and generally low unemployment and crime rates. And although Austrians could once be faulted for their unwillingness to confront their nation's culpability for Nazism and the Holocaust, that too has changed in recent years, as public awareness of the country's role in both of those tragedies has deepened.

Nevertheless, over the past three decades, radical right-wing populism has been more electorally successful in Austria than perhaps anywhere else in western Europe. On December 4, in Austria's presidential election, voters delivered a clear victory to Alexander Van der Bellen, the former head of the left-wing Greens. Yet Norbert Hofer, the candidate of the right-wing populist Austrian Freedom Party, won some

46 percent of the vote, not only setting a new record for his party but also securing more support than any other western European right-wing populist group has ever achieved in a national election.

Hofer's defeat seemed to break a winning streak for populist and antiestablishment forces that has roiled the West over the past year. But if Austria's mainstream parties want to keep the Freedom Party from another strong showing in the next parliamentary election, they need to overcome the deadlock that has prevented them from introducing reforms so that they can stimulate the economy, combat unemployment, and get a handle on Austria's refugee and immigration policy.

FROM POLITICAL INTEGRATION TO SOCIAL EROSION

Austria is governed by a parliamentary coalition comprising the center-left Social Democrats and the center-conservative People's Party. These two parties and their immediate predecessors founded the Austrian Republic in 1918, presided over its reconstitution after World War II, and have ruled ever since, mostly through grand coalitions.

In recent decades, the combined vote share of the Social Democrats and People's Party has plummeted, from 91 percent in 1983 to about 50 percent in 2013. As those parties' popularity waned, the Freedom Party's growing strength and its political radicalism have often left the two mainstream parties no alternative but to continue their awkward coalitions with each other. This, in turn, has intensified the public's desire for change. (In 2000, the People's Party tried to break this cycle by forming a government with the Freedom Party, but the results were disastrous: the Freedom Party's inclusion in the coalition provoked international outrage, the imposition of bilateral sanctions on Austrian officials, a loss for the People's Party in the 2006 elections, and a sharp decline for the Freedom Party in the polls.)

Since both the Social Democrats and People's Party are staunchly pro-European, they have received most of the blame for the negative consequences of European integration, beginning with the unpopular austerity measures and structural adjustments Austria undertook upon its accession to the EU in 1995. The influx of eastern European migrants that followed the EU's enlargement around a decade later and the union's various recent crises have further eroded popular support for the EU. As a result, Austria is now one of the bloc's most Euroskeptical members.

European integration has eroded the social partnership that many Austrians credit with their prosperity.

In some respects, that fact reflects Austria's historically ambivalent attitude toward Europe. Austria has long been fiercely committed to neutrality—a position that many Austrians consider the foundation of their country's security and which helps explain why the country never joined the U.S.-led NATO alliance. For most of the postwar era, Austria also kept some distance from Western liberal capitalism, maintaining instead a system known as the "social partnership." Most Austrians credit that system, under which labor and capital cooperate over such issues as wage bargaining and business regulations within a government-supported framework, with their country's prosperity and strong welfare state.

Over the past two decades, European integration has eroded both of these positions. Austria now participates in the European Union's defense architecture, and European economic integration has exposed Austria to liberal market pressures and eroded some important aspects of its social partnership. The privatization of public enterprises and deregulatory pressure from Brussels have weakened the bargaining power of unions and increased the differences in wages and working conditions across industries.

At the same time, Austria's membership in the EU's single market has presented new economic opportunities, especially in central and eastern Europe, where Austria's cultural know-how and historical ties have helped it become one of the region's largest investors. But if the overall effects of EU membership were positive, they were also uneven. As Austria has become more prosperous, competitive, and culturally diverse, many blue-collar workers have lost their jobs, as have many Austrians without university degrees. Lower middle class Austrians and public sector workers have been hit by wage stagnation, and the cost of living, especially housing, has increased substantially.

Some 75 percent of Austrians were either angry with or disillusioned by their country's politics in 2011, and the public's lack of trust in Vienna appears not to have improved since then. Many in the country—not just those who support the Freedom Party—also believe that their government has mishandled the migrant crisis. Over the past two years, the government has vacillated on that issue, first denying that migration presented a challenge worthy of special attention, then shifting to a more welcoming policy akin to that of Germany, and finally taking a harder line—one closer to the Freedom Party's—that will limit the number of asylum-seekers Austria accepts. That the country now faces uncharacteristically high levels of unemployment has made matters worse. The Freedom Party has managed to exploit all of these developments to its advantage.

THE BREXIT BACKLASH

Founded in 1956 by former Nazis and veterans of World War II, the Freedom Party languished for decades on Austria's far-right fringe before transforming into a right-wing populist party under Jörg Haider, the group's leader from 1986 until 2000. In recent decades, the party has campaigned on the idea that unaccountable and corrupt elites in Vienna and Brussels have failed to serve the Austrian people. It routinely portrays the country as threatened by mass immigration and violent crimes committed by foreigners. The Freedom Party advocates renationalizing issues now overseen by Brussels, such as the EU's freedom of movement policies, and supports transferring the responsibility for EU decision-making from supranational institutions to the bloc's member governments. In September, Heinz-Christian Strache, the party's current chief, called for Austria to join the Visegrad group, an alliance of Euroskeptical states that includes the Czech Republic, Hungary, Poland, and Slovakia.

Strache turned the Freedom Party rightward, securing a new, younger following.

Strache took control of the Freedom Party in 2005. At the time, the party was a member of the governing coalition with the People's Party and was on the verge of collapse because of an internal conflict between its more moderate leadership and its radical base. In an attempt to revive the party, Strache turned rightward. He harshly condemned the Austrian establishment and ramped up the party's xenophobic and Islamophobic rhetoric, declaring Islam incompatible with Austrian culture and implying an intrinsic connection between Islam and terrorism. The pivot helped the Freedom Party secure a new, younger following, much of it male and poorly educated, and shore up the party's base. Then, after a series of victories in regional and national elections in 2006 and 2008, the party sought to broaden its appeal and soften its image, putting up posters, for example, that called on Austrians to love their fellow citizens. In another instance, in 2014, the party forced its candidate for the European Parliament to withdraw from the race after he made a racist remark about a black Austrian soccer star. Strache also traveled to Israel several times in an effort to show that the party's anti-Semitism was a thing of the past. Hofer was an ideal figure to continue the mainstreaming of the party: he was a mild-mannered candidate who only hinted at the kinds of changes that the Freedom Party's victory would have brought.

Yet the Freedom Party lost anyway, due in part to a backlash in Austria against other recent populist victories in the West—particularly the United Kingdom's June vote to leave the EU, or Brexit, and the election of Donald Trump to the U.S. presidency. The fact that support among Austrians for European integration rose after the Brexit vote suggests that this is the case, as did the Freedom Party's efforts, toward the end of Hofer's campaign, to downplay its Euroskepticism and calls for change. Trump's election, meanwhile, may have unnerved some voters and helped propel Van der Bellen to victory.

Freedom Party leader Heinz-Christian Strache and presidential candidate Norbert Hofer at a rally in Vienna, May 2016.

MAINSTREAMED

In some respects, Hofer's defeat was a major setback for the Freedom Party. The presidency is a largely ceremonial post, but it carries some important powers. Austrian presidents can formulate political goals, rally voters, conduct their own foreign policies through invitations and state visits, and pressure or embarrass the government by withholding their signature from international agreements. Presidents can dismiss the government at will, and the chancellor, who leads the government, requires the president's approval to be appointed. Winning the election would have allowed Hofer to undermine Austria's fragile coalition government and sabotage its pro-European foreign policy.

The upside for the Freedom Party is that its loss may improve its chances in the next parliamentary elections, which are expected to be held by 2018. The party's current position should let it run as an outsider against the broad alliance of establishment forces that rallied behind Van der Bellen, especially since it stands far ahead of other parties in national opinion polls. In five of Austria's nine states, surveys suggest that the Freedom Party is either the most or second-most popular party.

Whether Austrians' desire for change or their fear of instability will prevail in the next election remains to be seen. In the meantime, the government has to deliver a series of reforms that will stimulate the economy, lower annual deficits, reduce the tax burden on wages, and improve the school system. Above all, it must present a comprehensive strategy for the integration of asylum-seekers. The mainstream parties' success is likely also to depend on the political performance of two figures who recently entered the political arena: Christian Kern, Austria's new Social Democratic chancellor, who is far more popular than any other party leader in the country; and Sebastian Kurz, the talented 30-year-old foreign minister from the Austrian People's Party, who is the country's most popular political figure and may soon take the helm of his own party. Both Kern and Kurz have suggested that they may be willing to push their respective parties toward cooperating with the Freedom Party. They have taken positions that resonate with Freedom Party voters, vowing, for example, to block Turkey's accession to the EU. For the first time since the 1980s, then, the Social Democrats, the Freedom Party, and the People's Party are all potential coalition partners for one another— despite Norbert Hofer's loss.

REINHARD HEINISCH is Professor of Austrian Politics in a Comparative Perspective and Chair of the Department of Political Science at the University of Salzburg. He is the co-author, with Oscar Mazzoleni, of *Understanding Populist Organization: The West European Radical Right*.

Europe's Hungary Problem

Viktor Orban Flouts the Union

R. Daniel Kelemen

A migrant holds his child on the Serbian side of the fence in Asotthalom, Hungary, September 2015.

Just as one rotten apple can spoil a barrel, one brutish autocrat can spoil a political union. As Hungarian Prime Minister Viktor Orban has consolidated power and built an increasingly authoritarian regime, he has thumbed his nose at the European Union—and mostly gotten away with it. Over the past few years, Orban has been a mild embarrassment for the union, but in his callous and shortsighted reaction to the ongoing refugee crisis, he has become a disgrace.

Styling itself as the defender of Europe's so-called Christian civilization against an Islamic invasion, Orban's regime has left thousands of refugees to languish in fields and in the streets, forcibly herded others into squalid detention camps, and fired water cannons and teargas at refugees gathered against the razor wire fence Hungary has erected on its border with Serbia.

European civilization may in fact be at risk. But it is Orban and his regime, not the desperate men, women, and children marching along the highway from Budapest to Vienna, who pose the real danger. The European Union claims to stand for liberal democracy, respect for human dignity, and human rights. With his regime's xenophobic rhetoric and hostile treatment of refugees, Orban is making a mockery of these values and encouraging other eastern European governments to follow his example.

Likewise, Orban is a threat to Europe's legal order. The Orban government claims that it is abiding by the EU's Dublin Regulation, set of rules governing how member states should process asylum claims, and that it is fulfilling its legal obligation to secure the EU's external borders. But the Orban government is distorting the application of these rules to pursue its populist, anti-immigrant agenda and is violating other EU rules concerning the humane treatment of refugees.

A BROKEN SYSTEM

Orban is right about one thing: The refugee crisis has revealed that the EU rules on immigration and asylum are in desperate need of reform. Under the Dublin system, the European Union places most of the burden for processing and caring for asylum seekers on the border states in the east and south, where migrants first enter the union and are supposed to make their asylum claims. This system is unfair and unsustainable. It places the bulk of the burden on poorer member states, such as Greece and Hungary, which are least equipped to handle it.

European civilization may in fact be at risk. But it is Orban and his regime, not the desperate men, women, and children marching along the highway from Budapest to Vienna, who pose the real danger.

The system also creates perverse incentives. Governments on the frontlines may be tempted to take a beggar-thy-neighbor approach, making themselves as unwelcoming as possible in the hope that migrants will seek asylum elsewhere. The migrants have incentives to break the EU rules and delay making asylum claims until they arrive in wealthier, more welcoming countries, such as Germany. And these more generous and humane governments may feel compelled to flout the rules and accept the refugees that they see suffering in states like Hungary.

The chaos unfolding across the EU's borders in recent weeks demonstrates that this system is unsustainable.

But for national leaders, such as Orban, to blame the European Union for such failures is the height of hypocrisy. In the first place, the Dublin rules were established with the agreement of EU member governments. Moreover, the European Commission has proposed—first in May and again this month—a new system of mandatory burden-sharing, in which all member states would agree to take in a quota of the refugees, determined on the basis of the country's size and wealth. France, Germany, Italy, and a handful of others support this approach, but Hungary has led a coalition of Eastern European states—alongside the increasingly isolationist United Kingdom—in opposing it.

Put simply, Orban has blocked sensible reforms of the EU's immigration and asylum system and then complained about its failings. His government creates as hostile an environment as possible for asylum seekers and then feigns dismay when they refuse to register their asylum claims in Hungary, as the EU's Dublin rules require.

BERNADETT SZABO / REUTERS

Hungarian policemen detain a Syrian migrant family after they entered Hungary at the border with Serbia, near Roszke, August 28, 2015.

VIKTOR VICTORIOUS?

Orban's controversial response to the refugee crisis is the latest chapter in his regime's ongoing defiance of EU norms. Over the past few years, as he has attacked Hungary's judicial independence and media pluralism, manipulated its electoral system, and otherwise consolidated his unchecked, one-party rule, the European Union has tried to restrain him, but only half-heartedly. The European Parliament has issued critical reports and the European Commission has launched legal actions against the Hungarian government for various violations of EU law. But none of it has been enough to deter Orban.

Some European leaders have criticized Orban's most provocative moves—such as his promise, in July 2014, to build an "illiberal state" along the lines of China, Russia, and Turkey, or his recent suggestion that Hungary should consider reintroducing the death penalty. But most leaders have failed to denounce him.

Orban's controversial response to the refugee crisis is the latest chapter in his regime's ongoing defiance of EU norms.

Left unchecked, it is impossible to predict how far Orban will go. Earlier this month, he used the migrant crisis to push a draconian immigration law through the Hungarian parliament. The law criminalized damaging or simply crossing a border blockade, such as the new fence on the border with Serbia, thus giving the government cause to arrest most asylum seekers entering the country. The law also empowered the government to declare a "state of migration emergency," which it did on September 15. The Orban government has started arresting and deporting migrants who cross the border fence. The government is processing asylum claims in special "transit zones" at the border, and rejecting and deporting applicants who have passed though Serbia, which Hungary has deemed a "safe country." The United Nations' High Commissioner for Refugees, Antonio Guterres, has called Hungary's policies "legally, morally, and physically unacceptable." The government has announced plans to extend the fence along Hungary's borders with EU member states Romania and Croatia, and the Hungarian parliament is set to consider granting the armed forces and police a range of new powers during migration emergencies.

STOP THE ROT

Europe must recognize the threat that the Orban regime poses to its democratic union. The refugee crisis not only demonstrates that the EU immigration and asylum system is broken, it also shows that no system can hope to function if a hostile member state actively seeks to undermine it. The Orban government's latest actions have violated the EU's core values of respect for human rights and human dignity, they have antagonized neighboring countries, and they have sown discord within the union. As EU leaders work in the coming days and weeks to replace the failed Dublin regime with a workable asylum and immigration regime that shares the burden fairly, they must also address the Orban problem.

The European Union should use all legal tools at its disposal to challenge the Orban government. Routine "infringement procedures," cases brought for isolated violations of EU law, have proven inadequate as they miss broader patterns of abuse. So the European Commission should consider bundling together a number of such cases into a so-called "systemic infringement action," which would demonstrate that the country in question—in this case Hungary—is engaged in a systemic breach of the EU's fundamental values.

MARKO DJURICA / REUTERS

A migrant prays near the border fence with Hungary in Horgos, Serbia, September 2015.

The European Union should also invoke Article 7 of the Treaty on European Union, which would enable it to suspend Hungary's voting rights within the EU for persistent, systematic violations of the union's fundamental values.

Legal tools should be backed by stiff financial penalties. As some European foreign ministers have suggested, the European Union should go beyond its normal procedures for fining states that violate EU law and consider suspending some of the funding Hungary receives from the EU. Orban bristles at EU criticism, but he is happy to take the EU's money. Indeed, his regime depends on it. Hungary contributes less than one billion euros to the EU's budget, but receives nearly 6 billion euros in EU funding, with total EU spending in Hungary amounting to more than 6 percent of its gross national income. More than 95 percent of all public investment projects in Hungary are co-financed by the EU. The union thus finds itself in the absurd position of heavily financing a regime that regularly attacks it.

But legal and financial tools alone may not be enough to stop Orban, whose government has demonstrated its facility at skirting EU rules even as it claims to comply with them. If national leaders across Europe want to stop Orban from antagonizing and fragmenting their union, they also need to apply direct political pressure on his regime.

All of Europe's leaders should stand together to publicly condemn Orban's rhetoric and policies. If they fail to do so, the rot will only spread.

To date, the most vocal criticism of Orban has come from leaders on the left of the political spectrum, such as Austria's Chancellor Werner Faymann. By contrast, leaders on the Center–Right have mostly kept silent or actively defended Orban. Why? Party politics. Orban's Fidesz party remains a member of the European People's Party—the coalition of Center–Right parties in the European Parliament— and his EPP colleagues have been reluctant to attack one of their own. In fact, with partisan interests in mind, leading EPP figures have publicly defended Orban.

This needs to stop. While many on the Center–Right may agree that tougher border controls and less inviting asylum policies are needed, they need to make it clear that Orban's treatment of refugees is beyond the pale. Leaders of the EPP, including German Chancellor Angela Merkel, Commission President Jean Claude Juncker, and Council President Donald Tusk, should begin by denouncing Orban's actions and announcing that his party will be ejected from their Center–Right coalition if his regime does not change course. Then all of Europe's leaders should stand together to publicly condemn Orban's rhetoric and policies. If they fail to do so, the rot will only spread.

R. DANIEL KELEMEN is Professor of Political Science and Jean Monnet Chair in European Union Politics at Rutgers University.

© Foreign Affairs

Europe's Autocracy Problem

Polish Democracy's Final Days?

R. Daniel Kelemen and Mitchell A. Orenstein

Law and Justice party leader Jaroslaw Kaczynski speaks at a pro-government demonstration in front of the Constitutional Court building in Warsaw, Poland, December 2015.

Winter has come to Europe, but it seems to be springtime for the continent's autocrats. Following the example of the Hungarian Prime Minister Viktor Orbán and his Fidesz Party, Poland's new government, led by the nationalist-populist Law and Justice party (PiS), has launched assaults on the country's judiciary and public media, putting Polish democracy and the rule of law at risk. In December, tens of thousands of Poles demonstrated against the government's illiberal actions; European Commission officials, meanwhile, have promised to investigate whether the developments in Poland constitute a "systemic threat" to the rule of law there. Unsurprisingly, Jaroslaw Kaczynski, the leader of the PiS, has dismissed the protestors as traitors and rejected criticism from abroad.

Poland's constitutional order is locked in a standoff.

In Poland's political crisis, the European Union is reaping the consequences of its inaction against Hungary's drift toward authoritarianism over the past five years. By failing to aggressively counter Orban's grab for power, the European Union signaled to aspiring autocrats across the continent that they could commit similar attacks on democracy and the rule of law without facing meaningful consequences. Clearly, Poland's PiS took note and has acted accordingly. If the European Union allows a second, much larger state to turn away from pluralist democracy and the rule of law, then the EU's standing as a union of democracies and a beacon for liberty in the region will be damaged irreparably. European Union leaders need to act quickly and forcefully to help preserve liberal democracy in Poland by making it clear that the country could face costly sanctions, including the suspension of EU funding, if the PiS-led government does not respect democratic principles.

A CONSTITUTIONAL CRISIS

The current crisis began with an illegal move by Poland's previous government, led by the liberal Civic Platform party, to exert influence over the Constitutional Court, a 15-member body that judges the constitutionality of legislation passed by Poland's parliament. Not content with only appointing replacements for three Constitutional Court judges who retired in November, the outgoing government also sought to appoint replacements for two judges who were set to retire after their terms expired in December, by which point a new government would have taken office. On December 3, the Constitutional Court struck down the latter two appointments, but held that the three judges appointed in November should take their seats on the Court.

An anti-government demonstration in front of the Constitutional Court in Warsaw, December 2015.

The story could have ended there, with the swearing in of three judges appointed by the Civic Platform in November and the selection of two other judges by the new PiS government. But by the time PiS took power in mid-November, it was in a combative mood. Throughout November, the PiS-backed President Andrzej Duda refused to swear in judges appointed by the previous Civic Platform government, blocking them from taking office. Rather than waiting for the Constitutional Court to rule on the validity of the appointments, the PiS-led parliament declared all five appointments invalid and appointed five replacement judges of its own. Then, the night before the Constitutional Court was set to rule on the validity of the originally appointed judges, Duda hurriedly swore in PiS' replacements. (Rejecting this brazen defiance of its authority, the Constitutional Court has refused to hear cases together with the PiS' illegitimate replacement judges.) Finally, in late-December, parliament passed a law designed to further hamstring the court, requiring, among other provisions, that at least 13 of its 15 judges be present to hear most of cases. Because there are only ten uncontested judges on the Court today, the law effectively precludes the body from hearing cases until it accepts the new government's replacement judges.

Poland's constitutional order is thus locked in a standoff, pitting the parliament and the president against the Constitutional Court: parliament has appointed five judges that the Constitutional Court does not recognize, whereas the Court recognizes three judges legitimately appointed by the previous government, whom the president and parliament refuse to recognize in turn. Kaczynski has made no secret of the agenda behind PiS' attack on the Court: at a mid-December rally, he stated plainly that he viewed the Court as a potential impediment to PiS delivering on its electoral promises, which include popular economic measures that will increase family benefits and lower the retirement age. But the deeper goals behind the party's attack on the Court are likely more far-reaching and worrisome: to prepare the ground for a raft of legislation that will curtail individual rights and distort democratic institutions, making it difficult to unseat PiS from power.

BUDAPEST IN WARSAW

By defying the Constitutional Court, weakening its mandate, and attempting to pack it with party loyalists, Kaczynski and the Law and Justice Party are following the example set by Hungary's Orban and his Fidesz party, which transformed Hungary into a semi-authoritarian state under the nose of the European Union. After Fidesz swept to power in 2010, Orban's government launched a constitutional revolution to eliminate independent checks on its power and consolidate Fidesz's rule for years to come. Hungary's powerful Constitutional Court, like Poland's, posed a threat to this agenda, and it became one of Orban's first targets. In 2010, the Orban government changed the procedure for appointing judges to allow the governing majority to make appointments without consulting the opposition. The next year, in 2011, the government adopted a new constitution that expanded the Constitutional Court from 11 to 15 judges, enabling Orban to pack it with Fidesz loyalists. When the Court nevertheless continued to declare some of the Orban's most egregious acts unconstitutional—among them, a law criminalizing homelessness and another requiring churches to secure official recognition through a vote in parliament—his government responded by amending the Constitution in 2013 so as to further limit the Court's power, granting constitutional status to a number of the laws the Court had declared unconstitutional, nullifying more than 20 years of the Court's case law, and further entrenching the control over the judiciary of the politically appointed head of Hungary's National Judicial Office.

Jaroslaw Kaczynski speaks with Polish President Andrzej Duda at the presidential palace in Warsaw, November 2015.

But Orban didn't stop with the courts. He also asserted control over independent public bodies that might check the government's power, reorganizing and replacing the heads of the Supreme Court, the ombudsman for data protection, the National Election Commission, and the National Media Board; asserted political control over public and private media; attacked civil society organizations, including churches and NGOs critical of his government; and overhauled Hungary's electoral system so that it would favor Fidesz. Although the European Commission, the European Parliament, and the Council of Europe have challenged a number of the Orban government's actions, EU institutions have so far failed to stop Hungary's drift toward authoritarianism.

PiS' recent record suggests that it has Hungary in mind. (On January 6, Kaczynski and Orban met privately in southern Poland for around six hours.) In addition to attacking the Constitutional Court, Poland's government has also passed a number of laws that will strengthen the PiS' hold on power and undermine the country's democracy. On December 30, parliament passed a bill, denounced by the European Union and media rights organizations, which will sack the current heads of the state television and radio stations and allow the government to appoint new ones. Another piece of legislation introduced by PiS lawmakers is designed to allow the government to fire civil servants at will. Polish lawmakers have also introduced amendments to a law on the police and special security services that will significantly increase the government's ability to wiretap and spy on Polish citizens. That is especially worrisome under a government led by PiS, which has historically led politicized witch-hunts to cast its opponents as spies or communists.

Poland's relatively young democracy has survived numerous challenges since the 1990s—from illiberal presidential candidates to constitutional reforms—and its adherence to democratic principles has secured the country a privileged place in the West and in the European Union, bringing about a period of sustained peace and prosperity rarely seen in the country's history. PiS' subjugation of the Constitutional Court and its disregard for the rule of law put all of that at risk.

"THE WORST SORT OF POLES"

PiS won Poland's October election in large part because it convinced Poles that, once in power, it would not be as extreme or combative as it was during its last period in government, from 2005 to 2007. At the time, PiS allied with extreme nationalist and populist parties in parliament and undertook a controversial witch-hunt to "de-communize" Poland by rooting out people (mostly opponents of PiS) who had allegedly collaborated with the former communist-era secret police, dramatically expanding domestic wiretapping to support its investigations.

Those moderate Poles who voted for PiS expecting that it would govern with greater restraint this time around were fooled. Public opinion polls show that many of these moderate voters have already changed their minds about PiS: 56 percent of Poles now believe that democracy is under threat in their country. Indeed, it is possible that PiS is gearing up for a four-year campaign against corrupt officials and perceived enemies of the state. PiS believes that the communists are at the root of most of Poland's ills, and it wants to remove communist-era secret police collaborators from government and most other areas of public life, from universities and the media to the military and public companies. With Antoni Macierewicz, an ardent anti-communist, as minister of defense, the inquisitions could be intense and protracted. Some of the language PiS has recently used to describe its opponents points in such a direction: Kaczynski has referred to his opponents as traitors, Gestapo agents, and "the worst sort of Poles" (najgorszy sort Polakow), a phrase that has become a popular t-shirt slogan and an Internet meme.

PiS' targets may not be limited to alleged former communists. The party wants to re-open an investigation into the death of Kaczynski's brother, former Polish President Lech Kaczynski, in a 2010 plane crash at a Russian military airport in Smolensk, which PiS claims was orchestrated by Russia and covered up by Poland's then-liberal government under Prime Minister Donald Tusk, who is now the president of the European Council. If the PiS investigates Tusk, it will effectively put the European Union itself on trial.

DEFENDING DEMOCRACY

Given the number of daunting challenges Europe faces—a potential British exit from the European Union; the arrival of large numbers of refugees and migrants; and the slowly festering eurozone crisis among them—it would be easy for European leaders to overlook Poland's internal battle over constitutional politics. Doing so, however, would be a profound mistake. If the European Union fails to defend democracy and the rule of law in Poland, as it did in Hungary, it will lose credibility as a union of pluralist democracies and risk encouraging a wave of democratic backsliding in other member states.

Of course, as the European Union's flawed record in Hungary has shown, protecting democracy in Poland will not be easy. This is mostly because the Union lacks adequate legal tools to address democratic backsliding. Article 7 of the Lisbon Treaty does enable EU member governments, acting unanimously, to strip another state of EU voting rights for serious and persistent violations of the EU's fundamental values including democracy, the rule of law, and respect for human rights—but with Poland and Hungary both drifting toward authoritarianism, Article 7 proceedings against either state would surely fail, as each country would shield the other from a unanimous vote. What is more, because European Council President Donald Tusk is a former Polish prime minister and longstanding enemy of Kaczynski, the PiS would have an easy time characterizing EU action against Poland as an opportunistic play by its domestic rivals.

Nevertheless, the European Union is not powerless to bring about change in Poland. Indeed, many of the political obstacles to EU action against Hungary do not exist with respect to Poland. Some leaders of the powerful European People's Party (EPP), a pan-European coalition of center-right parties of which Fidesz is a member, for example, have shielded Orban from criticism within the European Union. But PiS does not have the same advantage—the party is not a member of the EPP, and Kaczynski has fewer supporters in foreign capitals than Orbán does. That should make it easier for EU leaders to agree to act in the Polish case.

---

56 percent of Poles now believe that democracy is under threat in their country.

What is more, despite its failure to prevent the drift toward authoritarianism in Hungary, the European Union has shown elsewhere that it can protect democracy and the rule of law in member states. During Romania's 2012 constitutional crisis, for example, the EU quickly threatened the country with serious sanctions—including blocking its accession to the Schengen free movement zone—and successfully pressured Romanian Prime Minister Victor Ponta to back down from his attacks on the country's Constitutional Court and his efforts to impeach his rival, Romanian

President Traian Basescu. The European Union should act just as quickly and forcefully against Poland's current government—before PiS consolidates its grip on power.

The European Commission should begin by deploying its so far untested Rule of Law Mechanism, which provides for an escalating series of warnings in preparation for a vote on Article 7 of the Lisbon Treaty. But given the difficulty of stripping Poland of EU voting rights under Article 7, this will not be enough. EU leaders also need to consider suspending the flow of EU structural funds to Poland, currently Europe's largest recipient, unless the PiS government respects the requirements of EU membership. The United States should likewise pressure the Polish government, which is keen to strengthen NATO's presence in Poland and is set to host a NATO summit this year, by making it clear that it expects its ally to adhere to democratic values.

More broadly, if the European Union is to halt democratic backsliding and attacks on the rule of law in Poland and Hungary, the leaders of other EU member states will need to summon the political courage to speak out in defense of the EU's core values. Silence implies consent, and there has been too much silence in European capitals as democracy has eroded in Budapest and Warsaw. It is time for European leaders to signal to governments and citizens in both countries that a failure to respect the conditions of EU membership, above all pluralist democracy and the rule of law, will have real consequences.

R. DANIEL KELEMEN is Professor of Political Science and Law and Jean Monnet Chair in European Union Politics at Rutgers University. MITCHELL A. ORENSTEIN is Professor of Central and East European Politics at University of Pennsylvania.

www.ingramcontent.com/pod-product-compliance
Lightning Source LLC
Chambersburg PA
CBHW081150270326
41930CB00014B/3100